45743

INTERNATIONAL CAPITAL MOBILITY
AND EXTERNAL ACCOUNT DETERMINATION

International Capital Mobility and External Account Determination

A. J. Makin
Senior Lecturer in Economics
University of Queensland

St. Martin's Press

First published in Great Britain 1994 by
THE MACMILLAN PRESS LTD
Houndmills, Basingstoke, Hampshire RG21 2XS
and London
Companies and representatives
throughout the world

A catalogue record for this book is available
from the British Library.

ISBN 0–333–61343–0

Printed in Great Britain by
Ipswich Book Co Ltd
Ipswich, Suffolk

First published in the United States of America 1994 by
Scholarly and Reference Division,
ST. MARTIN'S PRESS, INC.,
175 Fifth Avenue,
New York, N.Y. 10010

ISBN 0–312–12100–8

Library of Congress Cataloging-in-Publication Data
Makin, A. J.
International capital mobility and external account determination
/ A. J. Makin.
p.   cm.
Includes bibliographical references and index.
ISBN 0–312–12100–8
1. Investments, Foreign.   2. Balance of payments.   3. Balance of
trade.   I. Title.
HG4538.M335   1994
332'.042—dc20   93–44094
                                                          CIP

To Fay

Contents

List of Figures

List of Tables

Preface and Acknowledgements

This book evolved from my experience as an economist in the Balance of Payments Section of the Australian Treasury in the mid-1980s. During those years, the current account balances and international investment positions of many OECD nations changed dramatically and, in some cases, became the main focus of macroeconomic policy. At the time it seemed strange to me that in an increasingly integrated global economy, characterised by greater mobility of capital across national boundaries, external imbalances should be considered problematic, in and of themselves. My view, consistent with the orthodox Humean perspective, was that external imbalances were essentially self-correcting and should not be macroeconomic policy targets. For reasons still somewhat unclear, such ideas suddenly became heretical. It is hoped that in part this book may contribute to establishing as orthodox about external imbalances what in many quarters, academic and official, is still deemed heterodox.

I would like to thank John Pitchford and Graeme Wells of the Australian National University, Ian Harper of the University of Melbourne, Bill Norton of Macquarie University and Giovanna Davitti of Macmillan for their comments on draft chapters. These individuals do not necessarily share my views about the significance of the external accounts, and the usual caveat applies about possible remaining errors in the analysis of this book. Last, but not least, thanks to Robyn McDonald, Margaret Cowan and Caroline Williams for typing and retyping the manuscript, Tanya Ziebell for library assistance and Brenda Marshall for suggestions on style.

A.J. MAKIN

1 Introduction

This book examines the causes and consequences of changes in nations' external account imbalances over recent decades. Contrary to suggesting these imbalances are a source of concern, a major aim of the book is to highlight the international macroeconomic gains which can result from increased international trade in saving.

1.1 THE INTERNATIONAL FINANCIAL ORDER

The economic significance of external account outcomes depends in part on prevailing exchange rate arrangements, as well as the extent of international capital controls. To put current international financial arrangements in historical perspective, let us first consider the evolution of the international monetary system to the present day. The historical development of the international monetary order is summarised in Table 1.1 below.

Table 1.1   A chronology of the international monetary order[1]

Late 1800s	Gold standard
1914–1918	World War I
1919–1925	Fluctuating exchange rates
1925–1931	Restored gold standard
1931–1940	Managed exchange rates, disorder
1940–1945	World War II
1945–1971	Bretton Woods era
Early 1970s	Flexible exchange rates

The gold standard is usually dated from the later part of the nineteenth century, when the main industrial economies of Europe and North America defined their currencies in terms of gold, though some of these countries had used gold for international settlements from much earlier times.

During World War I the gold standard was suspended and afterwards the currencies of Britain, France and many other nations floated quite freely until returning to the old rules from the mid-1920s. From the

1

early 1930s, many countries again abandoned gold and through to the end of World War II the international monetary system was characterised by economic nationalism, competitive devaluations and the proliferation of trade barriers and capital controls.

In light of the experience of the 1930s, delegates from 44 nations met at Bretton Woods, New Hampshire, in 1944 to produce the Articles of Agreement of the International Monetary Fund (IMF). This new set of rules (the Bretton Woods system) included the maintenance of stable exchange rates with the value of the United States dollar in terms of gold playing a pivotal role. The system broke down from the early 1970s, however, when the external value of the United States dollar could no longer be sustained. Thereafter, the exchange rates of leading industrial nations were essentially determined in foreign exchange markets.

In the wider international context, the presumption throughout the Bretton Woods era that free international trade in goods was to be encouraged did not extend to financial assets and no institutional framework analogous to the General Agreement on Tariffs and Trade (GATT) was established to negotiate on government-imposed impediments to capital movements.

The panoply of exchange controls of earlier decades reflected a somewhat xenophobic view of foreign money which especially prevailed during the interwar period. John Maynard Keynes (1933) reinforced this view by writing that: 'Ideas, knowledge, science, hospitality, travel – these are the things which should of their nature be international. But let goods be homespun whenever it is reasonable and conveniently possible, and above all else let finance be primarily national' (quoted in Kindleberger, 1987, p.67). Still later, Keynes (1941, p.23) declared that 'nothing is more certain than that the movement of capital funds must be regulated'.[2]

Official attitudes to controlling international capital flows have changed dramatically since World War II. Whereas the IMF Articles of Agreement, reflecting earlier attitudes to financial capital movements tolerated exchange controls as a supplement to exchange rate management, in contrast, the Code of Liberalisation of Capital Movements, first drafted by the Organisation for Economic Cooperation and Development (OECD) in the 1960s, proposed that international capital movements be progressively freed.

With the breakdown of the Bretton Woods system of exchange rate management, and in accordance with the OECD Code, financial markets were progressively deregulated with implications for capital flows, the effectiveness of monetary and fiscal policy and nations' external accounts.

Over the 1980s, for instance, the current accounts of Australia and the United States, as a proportion of GDP, averaged significant deficits of around 5 per cent and 2 per cent, whereas Japan and West Germany each sustained surpluses of around 2 per cent. Such imbalances may seem large compared with, for instance, the 1930s, 1940s and 1950s, decades characterized by prohibitive exchange controls, or with the 1960s and 1970s, when controls became less stringent.

International financial market reforms, particularly since the early 1970s, essentially eliminated the host of regulatory controls over international capital movements imposed after World War II. Nonetheless, international funds may be no more mobile across borders today than in the relatively frictionless international environment of the late nineteenth century and the early decades of this century. For example, the flow of capital from the United Kingdom persistently averaged over 5 per cent of GDP between 1870 and 1913,[3] while the flow of capital into Canada reached a peak of 13 per cent of GDP between 1910 and 1913.[4]

Under the generalised system of floating exchange rates, policymakers in many OECD countries often interpret the traditional macroeconomic policy goal of external balance as balance on the current account of the international accounts. Over the same time that external account imbalances became a concern, global financial markets were also, not coincidentally, increasingly liberalised. This gave rise to substantially increased capital mobility, and national saving and investment rates were no longer as closely correlated as in earlier decades. These developments prompted a range of economic policy prescriptions to bring about external adjustment.

For example, the Economic Report of the President of the United States in 1987 argued that 'the principal challenge of policy coordination was to reduce present international payments imbalances in a manner that supported sustained, non-inflationary growth in the world economy' (p.120). The IMF (1989) and the Bank for International Settlements (BIS) (1989) expressed similar concerns.

That current accounts should be balanced presumes nations should be neither exporters nor importers of capital. Is this economically justifiable? Indeed, could increased capital outflows matching higher current account surpluses have benefited some countries, at the same time as greater capital inflows matching current account deficits benefited others?

1.2   PLAN OF THE BOOK

This book provides an alternative perspective to that often proposed in international policy circles on the significance of the external imbalances of recent years. The argument develops as follows. Chapter 2 introduces and extends the external accounting and measurement framework necessary for the subsequent theory and policy analysis.

As a first step towards providing an appropriate theoretical paradigm for evaluating the behaviour of nations' external accounts, Chapter 3 critically surveys the theoretical approaches which have hitherto dominated the international macroeconomics literature. These traditional approaches include the classical, elasticities, absorption, monetary and Mundell–Fleming models. The shortcomings of these models, particularly the limitations of the Mundell–Fleming, or open economy Keynesian, approach are highlighted before a wholly different class of models is considered in Chapter 4.

These alternative approaches, which include neoclassical foreign investment theory, intertemporal models and an international variant of loanable funds analysis, can be used to demonstrate the macroeconomic significance of capital mobility and the gains from international trade in saving. Capital-centred approaches provide key insights about the desirability or otherwise of external imbalances and also provide the foundations for the saving–investment paradigm, on which the remainder of the book is based.

Chapter 5 argues that increased global integration of financial markets facilitated the widening of external imbalances. It also examines some major influences on patterns of saving and investment, including national fiscal policies.

Chapter 6 concludes the book by considering some of the fallacies which have mistakenly justified the external imbalance as an explicit target of macroeconomic policy in some OECD economies.

2 The External Accounting Framework

2.1 INTRODUCTION

The primary purpose of this chapter is to outline the international macroeconomic accounting foundations for interpreting a nation's external accounts.

In an open economy, resident households, firms and governments are constantly linked through the prices and quantities of goods, services and financial assets they buy and sell from foreigners. Whenever funds are exchanged between a resident and non-resident entity, the transaction is recorded in the nation's external accounts as well as, but with opposite sign, in the corresponding accounts of the non-resident's country. Balance of payments accounting records a nation's international trade in goods, services and assets and is important because it indicates the size and direction of international borrowing. As a summary of all such transactions, the external accounts are a subset of the national accounts and hence are best considered in an international macroeconomic framework.

2.2 DEFINITIONS AND ACCOUNTING RELATIONSHIPS

This section defines the major macroeconomic aggregates frequently referred to in the remainder of this book and the national and international accounting relationships which link them. A thorough understanding of these preliminaries is important since they form the basis for much of the theoretical and policy discussion of later chapters.

2.2.1 Absorption, Income and the Current Account

In a closed economy, ex post the value of *gross domestic product* (Y) equals *gross national expenditure*. However, in an open economy, total spending by resident households and firms is the *absorption* of domestically produced goods and services (A), as well as goods and services produced abroad. The difference between residents' spending on domestically produced goods and total absorption is *imports* (M). *Exports* (X) on the other hand, represent foreign spending on domestic product and equal the difference between national product and residents' spending on locally produced goods and services. In sum, therefore, $Y \equiv A + (X - M)$. Accordingly,

$$Y - A = X - M \tag{2.1}$$

If absorption exceeds output, the *net exports balance* is in deficit (T).

Another important distinction used subsequently is that between gross domestic product and *national income* (Y_n). The difference between these aggregates is due to *net income paid abroad* (y_a), the bulk of which is interest and dividends on existing *net external liabilities*, and *consumption of fixed capital* or depreciation allowances (d) such that $Y_n = Y - y_a - d$. Further, the national accounting term, *national disposable income* (Y_d), is national income less *net transfers paid abroad* (t). Therefore, $Y_d = Y_n - t$. The *current account balance* (CAB) is defined as $CAB = T + y_a + t$. The CAB recorded in the external accounts corresponds to the entry *net borrowing abroad* (b) recorded in the national accounts except that net borrowing abroad does not include *undistributed income* (u) accruing overseas.

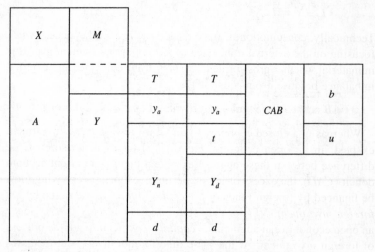

Figure 2.1   Absorption, income and the current account

The accounting relationships between the aggregates defined above, including gross domestic product, absorption, the trade balance, national income, national disposable income, the current account balance and net borrowing abroad are schematically depicted in Figure 2.1.

2.2.2 Saving, Investment and the External Accounts

We can now introduce the intertemporal dimension of national accounting by recognising that *gross saving* (*S*) is the difference between *gross national product* (*Y*) and *consumption* (*C*) whereas *gross domestic investment* (*I*) is the difference between total absorption and consumption. Hence

$$(Y - C) - (A - C) = S - I = X - M.$$

Therefore, when the trade balance is in deficit, not only must imports exceed exports, but gross investment must exceed gross domestic saving.

Domestic saving (S_d) is defined as the difference between national disposable income (Y_d) and consumption. Net domestic investment I_d is the difference between gross investment and depreciation allowances. From the above definitions, it follows algebraically that

$$S_d - I_d = X - M - y_a - t = CAB. \tag{2.2}$$

Technically, consumption of fixed capital (*d*) is of little concern when focusing on the external imbalance as the saving–investment gap. It is immaterial whether gross or net measures are used to measure external imbalance because, from equation (2.2),

$$CAB = S_d - I_d = (S - d) - (I - d) = S - I.$$

Whereas in a closed economy saving must always equal investment ex post, in an open economy the *CAB* provides a measure of the difference between these aggregates. When there is a current account deficit (*CAD*), the excess of net domestic investment over saving must be financed by foreign funds or *net capital inflow*, as measured by *net foreign investment* (*NFI*) or the *capital account surplus* (*KAS*). Hence an open economy can augment its *capital stock* (*K*) through the process of foreign investment. At the same time foreign investment increases the domestic economy's stock of net external financial liabilities.

The larger is the rise in the nation's capital stock, given the level of domestic saving, or the smaller is domestic saving or the addition to *national wealth* (W), given the increase in the capital stock, the larger is the *KAS*. In stock change terms, $dK - dW = KAS = NFI = CAD$ where the stock changes are net of capital gains and losses. Explaining net capital flows therefore also amounts to explaining changes in the stock of real capital goods relative to changes in national wealth levels.

By relying on foreign saving, as manifested in a capital account surplus, investment can therefore be greater than otherwise, for without foreign capital inflow, the level of domestic investment would be constrained by the pool of domestic saving. When foreigners finance expansion of the domestic capital stock, the rise in net external liabilities or *net international investment position* is therefore matched by an increase in the nation's real assets, although the cost of borrowing from foreigners eventually and sometimes almost immediately appears in the current account as income paid overseas. Income paid overseas can therefore be perceived as the return to foreigners for allowing an economy to expand its capital stock. Figure 2.2 represents the relationships between foreign saving, domestic saving and investment, the *national capital account*, and the external accounts.

A nation's NFI must be matched by a corresponding current account surplus experienced by the rest of the world (CAS^*), and this must also equal the rest of the world's capital account deficit (KAD^*) against the

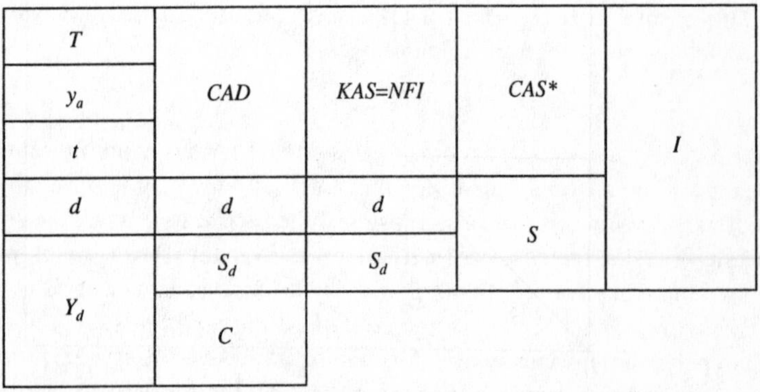

T				
y_a	CAD	$KAS=NFI$	CAS^*	I
t				
d	d	d	S	
Y_d	S_d	S_d		
	C			

Figure 2.2   Saving, investment and the external accounts

home economy. Figure 2.3 below depicts the accounting relationships between saving and investment at home and abroad and the international accounts.

Domestic saving (S_d) and net domestic investment (I_d) along with external saving (S') and net investment abroad (I') comprise world saving (S_W) and world investment (I_W). That is,

$$I_W = I_d + I' = S_W = S_d + S'.$$

Current and capital account imbalances therefore reflect regions' saving and investment patterns. That is,

$$I_d - S_d = NFI = CAD = KAS = S' - I' = CAS^* = KAD^*.$$

Only if domestic saving in each region fully finances domestic investment will the external accounts record a zero current or capital account balance. In Figure 2.3, this means external balance so defined includes all points on the 45° line.

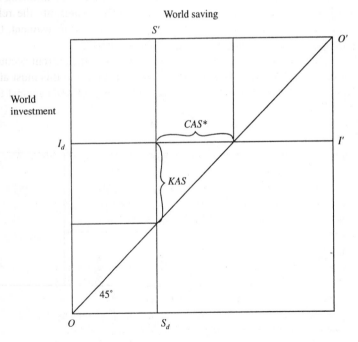

Figure 2.3   World saving and investment

However, when saving is free to cross international borders, domestic capital formation can be higher for a nation with a *KAS* whereas abroad capital formation is less than otherwise to the extent of CAS^*.

The discussion has so far assumed an economy without a public sector. However, the public sector through its public enterprises produces output and through its spending, taxing and borrowing also contributes significantly to national absorption and the demand for saving in an open economy. Total public absorption (G) is the sum of public consumption (C_g) and public investment (I_g). The budget, or public account imbalance, provides a measure of the gap between public saving (S_g) (the difference between net tax revenue (T_g) and public consumption expenditure (C_g)) and public investment expenditure (I_g). That is, the budget imbalance $= T_g - G = (T_g - C_g - I_g) = (S_g - I_g)$.

Private and public saving add up to domestic saving (S_d) as defined earlier since

$$Y_d - C_p - C_g = S_d = (Y_d - T_g - C_p) + (T_g - C_g) = S_p + S_g.$$

Since the external account imbalance is the domestic saving–investment imbalance

$$NFI = KAS = CAD = (I_p - S_p) + (I_g - S_g). \tag{2.3}$$

If the governments overall budget is balanced ($S_g = I_g$), *NFI* is solely attributable to the private sector's investment–saving imbalance.

2.2.3   Asset Markets and the External Accounts

Let us now explicitly introduce asset markets, financial instruments and the financial sector into a more general flow of funds framework. To further integrate the external accounts into the whole economic system and to extend our basic real framework by incorporating asset markets, consider the stylised accounting matrix in Table 2.1 below.[1] This matrix will be referred to in subsequent chapters outlining the major theoretical approaches to open economy analysis.

The matrix includes firms, households, the government, financial intermediaries and the central bank as the main sectors of the economy and records their economic and financial transactions with the rest of the world. Hence it adds to the earlier schema financial intermediaries (commercial banks and other financial institutions) and the central bank as agents in the macroeconomy. There are seven markets in which all

Table 2.1 Real and financial flows in an open economy

Market	(1) Households	(2) Firms	(3) Government	(4) Financial intermediaries	(5) Central bank	(6) Rest of the world	Total
(1) Goods and services	$-S_p$	I_p	$(I_g - S_g)$	—	—	CAB^*	0
(2) Money base	$dM_h^\dagger$	$dM_f^\dagger$	—	$dM_i^\dagger$	dM_r^-	—	0
(3) Bank deposits	$dD_h^\dagger$	$dD_f^\dagger$	—	dD_i^-	—	$dD^*_\ddagger$	0
(4) Bonds	$dB_h^\dagger$	$dB_f^\dagger$	dB_g^-	$dB_i^\dagger$	dB_r^+	$dB^*_\ddagger$	0
(5) Equities	$dE_h^\dagger$	$dE_f^\dagger$	—	—	—	$dE^*_\ddagger$	0
(6) Other debt instruments	$dH_h^\dagger$	dH_f^-	—	$dH_i^\dagger$	—	$dH^*_\ddagger$	0
(7) Foreign currency reserves	—	—	—	—	dR_r^+	$dR^*_\ddagger$	0
Total	0	0	0	0	0	0	0

real economic and financial transactions take place (the rows) as well as the six sectors (the columns). All rows and columns must sum to zero according to national and external accounting principles as well as balance sheet constraints.

Summing across the first row, $I_p - S_p + (I_g - S_g) = CAB^*$. Hence $(I_p - S_p) + (I_g - S_g) = NFI = CAD = KAS$ if public and private investment exceeds domestic saving as derived in equation (2.3). The remaining rows show, in simplified form, the various financial markets.

In the second row, changes in sectoral holdings of the money base (consisting of coin, banknotes and cash balances of the banks at the central bank) must reflect ex post changes in financial asset and liability positions. Assets are shown by superscript '+' and liabilities by superscript '−'. Assuming neither the government nor foreigners demand domestically issued base money, this row reveals that an increase in the base money supply, as a liability of the central bank, (dM_r^-) must be matched by a rise in money base held as an asset in the portfolios of firms (dM_f^+), households (dM_h^+) and financial inter- mediaries (dM_i^+). Hence $dM_f + dM_h + dM_i = dM_r$.

In the third row, a change in demand deposits with financial intermediaries can arise as deposits by households (dD_h^+), firms (dD_f^+) and foreign entities (dD_*^+) in financial intermediaries increase. The increased asset positions of households, firms and foreign entities is matched by a rise in the intermediaries' consolidated liability position such that $dD_f + dD_h + dD_* = dD_i$.

The fourth row simply shows that changes in the growth of government securities on issue, which are the liabilities of the central government, must be matched by increased holdings of bonds in the portfolios of the agents in the other five sectors. That is,

$$dB_h + dB_f + dB_i + dB_r + dB_* = dB_g.$$

Row five reveals that additional capital accumulation by private firms funded through the sale of equities must be absorbed as assets by households (dE_h) and foreign investors (dE_*). It is assumed that neither financial institutions nor the official sector is permitted to buy shares in domestic enterprises. Hence $dE_f = dE_h + dE_*$. If the enterprise issuing equities is a subsidiary of a foreign firm and new share issues are exclusively taken up by foreign buyers, then the item dE_* would be classified in the capital account as *direct* foreign investment in the economy. The distinction between direct and portfolio foreign investment is further discussed shortly.

The other main way of raising financial capital is through borrowing as shown in row six. This form of financing real capital accumulation also appears as a liability of domestic firms, but of course does not provide the lenders of funds with the same legal claim to ownership of domestic firms, as is the case with equity participation.

Firms may borrow either directly from households (dH_h) or foreigners (dH_*) (for instance, through the issue of company debentures) or alternatively they may borrow indirectly from those sectors through financial intermediaries (dH_i). Therefore $dH_f = dH_h + dH_* + dH_i$. If resident households provide insufficient funds to finance domestically located firms' investment activity, funds will be sought from abroad in the form of borrowings or equity participation. Though equity issues are usually denominated in domestic currency, foreign debt may be denominated in either domestic or foreign currency.

The last row shows the extent of foreign exchange market intervention undertaken by the central bank or the change in the stock of its official reserve assets (dR_*). Official reserve assets are by and large held in the form of financial assets previously issued by foreign governments and foreign central banks, but also include gold bullion. Hence $dR_r = dR_*$. Under a fixed exchange system, dR_*, as the change in the stock of official reserves, provides a measure of a nation's overall balance of payments position but, this measure of external balance effectively becomes redundant under a floating exchange rate system.[2] Instead, under a float, the change in official reserves provides a measure of the extent to which the central bank intervenes to prevent appreciation or perhaps induce depreciation of the exchange rate itself.

Next consider the columns of the matrix which present the budget constraints of all six sectors. In column one, households dispose of their saving by increasing holdings of cash balances, (dM_h), cash deposits (dD_h), bonds (dB_h), equities (dE_h) and interest bearing securities (dH_f). The total increase is the change in household wealth (dW_h). So

$$S_p = dM_h + dD_h + dB_h + dE_h + dH_f = dW_h.$$

Firms (column two) produce goods and services for sale in markets and finance additional net capital accumulation by issuing securities as claims in the form of equities (dE_f) and debt (dH_f) or by running down cash balances (dM_f) and bank deposits (dD_f), or by selling bond holdings (dB_f).[3] The total increase is the change in the capital stock of enterprises, dK_p. Hence

$$I_p = dE_f + dH_f - dM_f - dD_f - dB_f = dK_p.$$

Column three is the government's budget constraint. The government sector includes 'departments of State', but in practice often excludes public sector business enterprises which are usually grouped with private firms for data collection purposes. If there is a budget deficit, there is an excess of government investment spending (I_g) over public saving (S_g), and this deficit is financed by issuing government bonds. The government's net financing requirement is therefore $dB_g = I_g - S_g$.

The financial sector (column four) includes licensed trading, saving and development banks and non-bank financial institutions which incur liabilities and acquire financial assets. For financial intermediaries, the budget constraint is $dM_i + dB_i + dH_i = dD_i$ which states that changes in this sector's holdings of cash reserves (dM_i), bonds (dB_i) and its consolidated loan position (dH_i), all recorded on the credit side of the balance sheet, are equivalent to the change in deposits (dD_i), recorded on the debit side.

The fifth column is the central bank's budget constraint. It shows that the supply of base money can only be increased (dM_r) through the central bank's open market purchases of bonds (dB_r) or by purchases of foreign exchange or securities in the foreign exchange market. Hence foreign exchange market intervention has monetary consequences and may therefore be undertaken by the central bank as a means of expanding or contracting the money supply for macroeconomic stabilisation purposes. However, if influencing the exchange rate is the sole objective of intervention (dR_r), the change in the money base (dM_r) must be offset, or sterilised, through open market operations by an equivalent change in the central bank's bond holdings (dB_r). For instance, if the central bank buys foreign exchange to prevent appreciation of the exchange rate, it must simultaneously sell government bonds from its portfolio to prevent an unintended monetary expansion.

Finally, the sixth column shows the composition of net capital inflow from the perspective of the rest of the world, classified by financial instruments. Under a pure float, there is no central bank intervention in the foreign exchange market, so $dR_r = dR_* = 0$. As shown previously the rest of the world's net capital outflow is equivalent to the domestic economy's *CAD* or *NFI*.

NFI therefore arises because foreigners use their surplus saving to purchase equities (dE_*) and debt instruments (dH_*) issued by domestic firms, bonds (dB_*) issued by the government and by depositing funds with financial institutions (dD_*). Hence $NFI = dE_* + dH_* + dB_* + dD_*$. If the exchange rate is fixed or if the central bank intervenes in the foreign exchange markets, the change recorded in the stock of official reserve assets (dR_r) also changes the liability position of the rest of the world (dR_*). Any rundown of reserves which may be the result of a central bank strategy to appreciate the currency, or prevent it from depreciating, therefore augments the existing capital inflow which is financing the nation's *CAD*.

If the government's budget is balanced ($I_g - S_g = dB_g = 0$) and there is a pure float ($dR_r = dR_* = 0$), it follows from the matrix that foreigners can finance, through purchases of domestic equity, debt instruments and bank deposits, that much more private domestic capital accumulation; that is, $dD_* + dE_* + dH_* = dK_p$.

A further distinction drawn about *NFI* is that between *portfolio* investment and *direct* investment. Portfolio or indirect investment refers to ordinary foreign purchases of domestic debt or equity claims whereas direct foreign investment includes investment which suggests significant foreign control over the management of resident firms and their real assets including subsidiaries of foreign firms. For measurement purposes, foreign ownership of at least 10 per cent of ordinary shares or equivalent equity interest in an enterprise is defined as constituting significant influence. Schematically, the distinction is as shown in Figure 2.4.

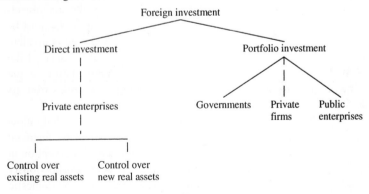

Figure 2.4   Direct vs portfolio foreign investment

2.2.4   National Wealth Accounting

So far, the main focus of this chapter has been the interrelationship between domestic and international macroeconomic flow magnitudes. However, the associated macroeconomic stock measures are also important since these permit measurement of national wealth in open economies.

To estimate open economies' wealth positions, it is necessary to construct national balance sheets. National balance sheets should be an integral part of national accounting. They are tied directly to aggregate flows through the national capital account which records saving and investment aggregates, these in turn having been derived from the income and product accounts. While total domestic investment equals domestic saving plus net capital inflow, national net worth or wealth equals tangible assets less foreign liabilities. As complements to the flow national income measures, national balance sheets complete the full System of National Accounts (SNA), as actually recommended by the United Nations.[4] They should include all assets and liabilities which have market values and can be expressed in dollar terms. In a globally integrated economic system, market values should, ideally, reflect the prices bid for domestic assets if these assets were offered for sale on international goods, services and financial markets.

In the international literature, Goldsmith and Lipsey (1963) first devised a balance sheet for the United States and thoroughly detailed the conceptual and practical problems that arise with macroeconomic stock estimation. Goldsmith (1985) later extended this approach and

Table 2.2   Stylised open economy balance sheet

Assets		Liabilities (claims on assets)
Consumer durables		Foreign liabilities
Capital stock		Private
Private		Public
Public		
Foreign assets		
Private		
Public		Residents' net worth (national wealth)
Total assets	=	Total claims

provided stylized balance sheets for twenty countries, stressing sectoral asset and liability positions but stopped short of identifying overall national wealth.

Taking the case of an internationally indebted open economy, national net wealth, is simply defined as the excess of the value of residents' assets, (comprised of consumer durables,[5] the tangible capital stock, and foreign assets), over external liabilities, as shown in the stylised balance sheet (Table 2.2) above.

2.3 MEASUREMENT PROBLEMS

In the foregoing discussion of the value of the balances in the external accounts, it was implicitly assumed that it was appropriate to measure external imbalances in domestic currency terms. However, there are valuation effects particularly on trade flows and servicing of foreign debt, which arise because of movements in the exchange rate. To provide a hypothetical example of this phenomenon, focussing on the trade balance, assume imports were $200m and exports $100m. The trade deficit would therefore be $100m. However, after a 50 per cent depreciation, import and export prices would rise by the same percentage amount and the trade deficit would become $150m, all other things constant. This valuation effect, sometimes referred to as a 'J curve' effect, is to some extent an arithmetic illusion due to the fact that following a currency depreciation, import values are affected by more in domestic currency terms than export values when starting from a trade deficit.

Such valuation effects suggest that a foreign currency measure of the imbalance may for some purposes provide a more meaningful measure of trends, particularly if we are concerned with the extent of capital flows from a foreign perspective, which is how column six of the real and financial flows matrix (Table 2.1) is actually presented. For instance, if a reason for concern about an ever-increasing *CAD*, as officially measured, is its effect on the sentiment of foreign investors themselves, or if it is necessary to gauge the extent of foreign currency saving being exchanged for domestically created assets, it seems logical to present the external imbalance in terms of foreign currency thereby largely abstracting from the exchange rate valuation effect.

In principle, since every international transaction recorded in one nation's external accounts should be debited on another's, the sum of external balances for the world as a whole should be zero. In practice, however, the world's external account does not balance, but tends to show a persistent deficit. Reasons for this include measurement errors other than valuation effects, relating to underrecorded interest credits from abroad.[6]

2.4 CONCLUSIONS

Taken as a whole, a nation's international transactions must always balance. Under a float, exchange rates themselves move to eliminate any excess demand or supply of currencies on the foreign exchanges whereas the central bank mops up any excess currency supply or demand through its exchange market intervention when exchange rates are officially managed. With a float, if one particular category of external transactions rises or falls, an equilibrating mechanism leads to an offset in other external account categories.

For example, if there is increased demand for an economy's financial assets, the additional foreign investment raises the capital account surplus which may strengthen the exchange rate, with offsetting implications for the trade balance. In sum, the current and capital account imbalances are jointly determined at the point where the net demand for foreign funds on one side matches the net supply on the other with the exchange rate proximately performing the equilibrating role.

The 'balance of payments' as such does not refer to the notion of the balance of payments as understood if the exchange rate is fixed. With a fixed exchange rate, the balance of payments is essentially the measure of the change in the central bank's holdings of foreign exchange reserves. Under the Bretton Woods system of exchange rate management nations' balance of payments problems most often involved unsustainable run-downs in official international reserve assets. Such holdings were necessary to maintain the value of the currency in the face of a shortfall between residents' demand for foreign currency arising, for example, as a consequence of the demand for imports, and the supply of foreign currency provided to residents by foreigners as occurred, for example, when exports were sold. When that system prevailed, international capital markets were far less sophisticated and financial capital flows were less voluminous; balance of payments deficits therefore usually arose for current account reasons though there were substantial international capital flows. Nevertheless, availability of central banks' reserves represented the ultimate external constraint on an economy's performance.

In contrast, the floating exchange rate system in operation from the early 1970s, almost by definition has not depended on direct foreign exchange market intervention by the monetary authorities to maintain any particular exchange rate. Under the purest of exchange rate floats, the overall balance of payments of a nation should in practice be zero with the exchange rate itself bearing all the pressure of external adjustment. Hence, in what follows the focus will not be the overall balance of payments as the measure of central bank intervention in the foreign exchange markets but the two matching sides of the external accounts – the current account and the capital account.

The macroeconomic notion of 'external imbalance' as a constraint was widely employed during the fixed exchange rate era, to describe external account outcomes characterised by either unsustainable rundowns or excessive accumulations of foreign currency reserves by central banks. However, with the progressive dismantling of capital controls, along with the shift to more flexible exchange rates, the old notion of external imbalance as a reserve constraint lost its former meaning. Nonetheless, the term persists in the literature and in popular usage but now generally refers to current account outcomes. Often, however, the term still conveys the implication that some form of remedial macroeconomic policy action is necessary. However, as will be argued in what follows in later chapters, such an understanding is misplaced under current circumstances. Therefore in this and subsequent chapters, whenever the term 'external imbalance' is used in discussing developments under floating exchange rates, it is simply meant to describe the current account outcome, capital account outcome, or net foreign investment position; it is not meant to convey a state of macroeconomic disequilibrium begging a particular macroeconomic policy response.

This chapter presented a detailed international macroeconomic accounting framework to be recalled in subsequent chapters. For instance, in Chapters 3 and 4, the many approaches to external account determination and capital movements are expounded and critically evaluated with frequent reference to the real and financial linkages detailed above.

3 Traditional Approaches to the External Accounts

3.1 INTRODUCTION

This chapter presents traditional approaches to external account determination by expositing and critically evaluating the main models which have surfaced over the years. The different approaches are presented largely in order of their chronological appearance. What becomes apparent is that economists' perceptions of the theoretical and policy significance of the external accounts evolved in line with changes in the international 'rules of the game' which characterised the international monetary system.

In the beginning, the classical adjustment mechanism sought to explain the dynamics of reaching external equilibrium with fixed exchange rates under the gold standard. After the abandonment of the gold standard, the elasticities approach to trade account adjustment became popular and was heavily influenced by the partial approach of Neo-classicism with its emphasis on changing relative prices of exports and imports, yet in an environment where the exchange rate could be used as an instrument of policy. After the emergence of macroeconomics as a distinct sub-discipline from the late 1930s, economy-wide approaches to the external accounts again became popular as reflected in the absorption related approaches of the 1950s.

In the 1960s, the monetary approach to the external accounts emerged in the open economy literature in parallel with the Monetarists' rejection of the Keynesian emphasis on the expenditure aggregates, to the neglect of monetary factors, in the closed economy literature. However, the rules of the game when these earlier approaches first emerged were managed exchange rates and limited international capital mobility. The macroeconomic approaches which developed in the two decades following World War II for instance, did so in an environment where strict exchange controls over the movement of financial capital were in force which effectively segmented financial markets, making capital markets unresponsive to interest rate differentials. Hence the models of this era used fixed exchange rates and capital immobility as starting assumptions such that the current account became the focus of balance of payments analysis to the disregard of the capital account. It was not until the 1960s, by which time capital markets had become more integrated, that the significance of capital mobility was fully recognised and explicitly modelled in the Mundell–Fleming approach. With the move to floating rates in the 1970s and 1980s, the flexible exchange rate–perfect capital mobility variant of the Mundell–Fleming approach came to the fore, largely because it was consistent with the international rules then prevailing.

Since we are most interested in the significance of the external accounts in an environment of floating exchange rates and capital mobility, the Mundell–Fleming approach, including recent extensions, is treated in more depth than its predecessors as it remains the prevailing orthodoxy in open economy macroeconomics. Nonetheless, we conclude that this mainstay approach falls short of providing a meaningful framework for analysing the macroeconomic implications of foreign investment flows, largely because of its ad hoc formulation of the current and capital accounts and its failure to capture common determinants of the external accounts taken as a whole.

3.2   THE CLASSICAL APPROACH

The open economy literature has traditionally focused on the trade and current account imbalance as a measure of balance of payments disequilibrium or external imbalance. Although the notion of external balance is today somewhat elusive under conditions where international borrowing and lending is freely permitted and exchange rates float, it was clear to the ancient Mercantilist school of thought, popularly espoused in England between the fifteenth and mid-eighteenth centuries, that external balance meant a trade surplus. The Mercantilist position on the balance of payments is best captured in Thomas Mun's (1664) pamphlet entitled 'England's Treasure by Foreign Trade, or the Balance of Our Foreign Trade is the Rule of Our Treasure' in which he proposed that: 'The ordinary means therefore to increase our wealth and treasure is by Foreign Trade, wherein we must even observe this rule: to sell more to strangers yearly than we consume of theirs in value.' Why a trade surplus was of itself beneficial was not clearly enunciated by the Mercantilist writers, although it was tied to their belief that the accumulation of specie was the chief means by which nations could increase their wealth.

The benefits or otherwise of particular outcomes on the trade account continue to generate debate. Indeed, Mercantilist instincts apparently live on in the hearts of many economists and policy makers today to the extent that external balance is often understood as achieving a surplus on the current account. Not only should the current account be an explicit goal of policy but, in the Mercantilist spirit, a current account surplus is somehow indicative of national economic welfare.

3.2.1 The Basic Model

Using a macroeconomic argument, David Hume discredited the Mercantilists' policy objective of actively pursuing a trade surplus and, in so doing, exposited the first theory of balance of payments adjustment. In his classic essay, 'Of the Balance of Trade' (1752) Hume outlined what became known as the 'price-specie-flow' mechanism under the gold standard.

The gold standard operated on the basis that the value of national currencies or base monies was defined in terms of gold. With gold as the internationally agreed standard of value, this implied that currencies were therefore defined in terms of each other. As payments imbalances arose, gold reserves could be physically transported across national borders to settle international accounts for goods bought and sold.

Hume argued that under the gold standard, a trade surplus would certainly induce gold inflow but this would also increase the domestic money supply. Through the quantity theory of money, the domestic price level would then rise, worsening competitiveness which would subsequently reverse the trade imbalance.

Schematically

(1)		(2)
Trade surplus (deficit)	➤	Gold inflow (outflow)

(3)		(4)
➤ Money supply increase (decrease)	➤	Domestic price level increase (decrease)

(5)		(6)
➤ Fall (rise) in competitiveness	➤	Reversal of trade surplus (deficit)

Importantly, the linkages suggested that trade account imbalances were eventually self correcting, thus obviating the need for any policy response to balance of payments disturbances.

Nonetheless, several factors could impede the external adjustment process proposed by Hume. For instance, the link between stages (3) and (4) has been the subject of continued controversy, particularly its relevance for short period analysis. Furthermore, the link between stages (5) and (6) also only worked with constant foreign price levels and the absence of retaliatory trade action on the part of foreign governments. The exact nature of the relative price conditions necessary at stage (5) to alter the trade imbalance at stage (6) later preoccupied the advocates of the so called elasticities approach.

3.2.2 Limitations

This approach can also be criticised on the grounds that it implicitly assumed wages and prices were fully flexible both upwards and downwards and that full employment of resources therefore prevailed. This assumption was of course subsequently at the heart of Keynes' (1936) challenge of classical orthodoxy.

Misplaced Mercantilist doctrine about the paramount importance of the trade account also provided Hume's contemporary, Adam Smith, with a motive for writing *The Wealth of Nations* (1776) in which Smith espoused the case for minimal intervention by government in most spheres of economic activity including trade with foreigners. Smith rejected the thrust of Mercantilist precepts and policy prescriptions, about the need for State intervention to improve economic welfare, yet his classic book does not acknowledge the price–specie–flow model, or anything resembling it. Instead, Smith emphasised the gains from international trade which hitherto had been largely considered as a zero sum game. On the question of external imbalance, Smith commented:

> Nothing ... can be more absurd than this whole doctrine of the balance of trade ... When two places trade with one another, this doctrine supposes that, if the balance be even, neither of them either loses or gains; but if it leans in any degree to one side, that one of them loses, and the other gains in proportion to its declension from the exact equilibrium. Both suppositions are false ... that trade

which, without force or constraint, is naturally carried on between any two places, is always advantageous ... to both. (Adam Smith, Bk. IV, Ch. III, part 2, para. 2)

This Smithian theme re-emerges when the gains from international trade in saving are considered in the next chapter.

Although it was the ruling orthodoxy until the abandonment of the gold standard in the early 1930s, whereafter it lost its immediate relevance, it was the Humean adjustment mechanism which profoundly influenced subsequent international monetary theory and balance of payments analysis. Indeed, as becomes clear later in this chapter, many elements of the approach resurfaced intact in the monetary approach to the balance of payments which became popular in the 1960s.

3.3   THE ELASTICITIES APPROACH

While the classical approach was the centrepiece of external adjustment theory during the neo-classical Marginalist revolution of the late nineteenth century, Marginalism, with its emphasis on partial, as opposed to general equilibrium analysis, inspired a new approach to the balance of payments termed the 'elasticities approach'. With the trade balance still the main focus, the elasticities approach explained the response of exports and imports, not under the classical conditions where the exchange rate was fixed by virtue of the gold standard and domestic price levels varied, but where domestic price levels were fixed and the exchange rate itself could vary. In common with the classical approach, the elasticities approach did not allow changing national income levels to affect trade flows. Instead, it sought to establish the conditions necessary for changes in competitiveness to improve trade imbalances.

The approach was based on contributions by Marshall (1923), Bickerdike (1920), Robinson (1937), Lerner (1944) and Harberger (1950). In essence, this perspective centred on the response to exchange rate changes of the trade balance in foreign exchange terms, since trade deficits ultimately had to be financed by depleting official foreign exchange reserves.

3.3.1 The Basic Model

The elasticities approach addressed the conditions necessary for devaluations to improve trade balances. These necessary conditions can be derived as follows:

The change in the trade balance is expressed as

$$dT^* = dX^* - dM^* \tag{3.1}$$

where asterisks here denote foreign exchange values.

Starting with the export side of the trade account, X^* can be further expressed as

$$X^* = Q_x P_x^* \tag{3.2}$$

where Q_x is the volume of exports and P_x^* is the foreign price of exports. If e is the price of foreign exchange, then

$$P_x = e P_x^* \tag{3.3}$$

where P_x is the domestic price of exports.

The elasticity of supply of exports with respect to price is

$$\varepsilon_x = \frac{dQ_x}{Q_x} \bigg/ \frac{dP_x}{P_x} \tag{3.4}$$

and the elasticity of demand for exports on the part of foreigners is

$$\eta_x = \frac{-dQ_x}{Q_x} \bigg/ \frac{dP_x^*}{P_x^*}. \tag{3.5}$$

From (3.3),

$$\frac{dP_x}{P_x} = \frac{de}{e} + \frac{dP_x^*}{P_x^*}. \tag{3.6}$$

Substituting (3.6) into (3.4), we obtain

$$\varepsilon_x = \frac{dQ_x}{Q_x} \bigg/ \left(\frac{dP_x^*}{P_x^*} + \frac{de}{e} \right). \tag{3.7}$$

Using (3.5) we also obtain

$$\frac{dQ_x}{Q_x} = -\eta_x \frac{dP_x^*}{P_x^*}. \tag{3.8}$$

Substituting (3.8) into (3.7)

$$\frac{dP_x^*}{P_x} = \left(\frac{-\varepsilon_x}{\eta_x + \varepsilon_x}\right) \frac{de}{e} < 0. \tag{3.9}$$

Substituting (3.9) back into (3.5)

$$\frac{dQ_x}{Q_x} = \left(\frac{\eta_x \varepsilon_x}{\eta_x + \varepsilon_x}\right) \frac{de}{e} > 0. \tag{3.10}$$

The proportionate change in the value of exports is

$$\frac{dX^*}{X^*} = \frac{dP_x^*}{P_x} + \frac{dQ_x}{Q_x}. \tag{3.11}$$

Substituting from (3.9) and (3.10) yields

$$\frac{dX^*}{X^*} = \frac{\varepsilon_x(\eta_x - 1)}{(\eta_x + \varepsilon_x)} \frac{de}{e}. \tag{3.12}$$

On the imports side, the foreign currency value of imports is

$$M^* = Q_M P_M^* \tag{3.13}$$

where Q_M is the volume of imports and P_M^* is the foreign price of imports. The domestic price of imports,

$$P_M = e P_M^*. \tag{3.14}$$

The elasticity of supply of imports with respect to price is

$$\varepsilon_m = \frac{dQ_M}{Q_M} \bigg/ \frac{dP_M^*}{P_M^*}. \tag{3.15}$$

The elasticity of demand for imports domestically is

$$\eta_M = \frac{-dQ_M}{Q_M} \Big/ \frac{dP_M}{P_M}.$$

(3.16)

From (3.14),

$$\frac{dP_M}{P_M} = \frac{dP_M^*}{P_M^*} + \frac{de}{e}.$$

(3.17)

Substitute (3.17) into (3.16)

$$\eta_M = \frac{-dQ_M}{Q_M} \Big/ \left(\frac{dP_M^*}{P_M} + \frac{de}{e} \right).$$

(3.18)

From (3.15)

$$\frac{dQ_M}{Q_M} = \varepsilon_M \frac{dP_M^*}{P_M^*}.$$

(3.19)

Substitute (3.19) into (3.18), to obtain

$$\frac{dP_M^*}{P_M^*} = \frac{-\eta_M}{(\eta_M + \varepsilon_M)} \frac{de}{e}.$$

(3.20)

Using (3.20) in (3.15) and solving for the proportionate change in the quantity of imports,

$$\frac{dQ_M}{Q_M} = \frac{-\varepsilon_M \eta_M}{(\varepsilon_M + \eta_M)} \frac{de}{e}.$$

(3.21)

Now the proportionate change in the value of imports is

$$\frac{dM^*}{M^*} = \frac{dP_M^*}{P_M^*} + \frac{dQ_M}{Q_M}.$$

(3.22)

Substituting from (3.20) and (3.21)

$$\frac{dM^*}{M^*} = \frac{\eta_M(\varepsilon_M + 1)}{(\varepsilon_M + \eta_M)} \frac{de}{e}.$$

(3.23)

Substituting the expressions in terms of elasticities derived for proportionate changes in exports (3.12), and proportionate changes in imports (3.23), into equation (3.1)

$$dT^* = \left[X^* \frac{\varepsilon_x(\eta_x - 1)}{(\eta_x + \varepsilon_x)} + M^* \frac{\eta_M(1 + \varepsilon_M)}{(\eta_M + \varepsilon_M)} \right] \frac{de}{e}.$$
(3.24)

With balanced trade, $X^* = M^*$, so that a devaluation $\left(\dfrac{de}{e} \right)$ only improves the trade balance if .

$$\frac{\varepsilon_x(\eta_x - 1)}{(\eta_x + \varepsilon_x)} + \frac{(\eta_M(1 + \varepsilon_M))}{(\eta_M + \varepsilon_M)} > 0$$
(3.25)

where, redefining for convenience, ε_x is the elasticity of the domestic supply of exports, η_x is the elasticity of foreign demand for exports, ε_M is the elasticity of the supply of imports and η_M is the elasticity of domestic demand for imports.

From (3.25) we can derive special conditions. For instance, consider first the case of a small economy facing an infinitely elastic foreign demand for its exports($\eta_x = \infty$) and an infinite supply of imports ($\varepsilon_M = \infty$). Taking the limit of (3.25)

$$\underset{\eta_x, \varepsilon_M \to \infty}{Lim} \left\{ \frac{\varepsilon_x(\eta_x - 1)}{(\eta_x + \varepsilon_x)} + \frac{\eta_M(1 + \varepsilon_M)}{(\eta_M + \varepsilon_M)} \right\} = \varepsilon_x + \eta_M > 0.$$
(3.26)

Hence, a devaluation always raises net exports for a small economy.

The next condition assumes underutilized capacity at home such that increased export demand is automatically met by exports, the supply of which is infinitely elastic ($\varepsilon_x = \infty$). Moreover there are no supply constraints abroad either, such that the supply of imports is infinitely elastic ($\varepsilon_M = \infty$). Taking the limit of (3.25) under these assumptions,

$$\underset{\varepsilon_x, \varepsilon_M \to \infty}{Lim} \left\{ \frac{\varepsilon_x(\eta_x - 1)}{(\varepsilon_x + \eta_x)} + \frac{\eta_M(1 + \varepsilon_M)}{(\varepsilon_M + \eta_M)} \right\} = \eta_x + \eta_M - 1 > 0.$$
(3.27)

(3.27) can be rewritten as $\eta_x + \eta_M > 1$, which is known as the Marshall–Lerner condition.

3.3.2   Limitations and Extensions

As an abbreviated form of the elasticities approach, the Marshall–Lerner condition therefore suggested that a devaluation of a country's currency would improve its trade or current account balance if the sum of the price elasticities of domestic and foreign demands for imports were larger than unity. This condition therefore ensured that the increased quantity of exports following a change in relative prices after a devaluation offset the increased cost of imports. If the condition was not met, this implied revaluation, not devaluation, was necessary for restoring external balance. The key assumption of the Marshall–Lerner variant of the elasticities approach was that the supply of exports and imports were infinitely elastic. Though the macroeconomic implications of changes in export and import volumes were not considered by the approach, implicitly the assumptions about supply elasticities were only applicable to recessed economies. Hence, in this regard, the approach was inconsistent with the full employment assumption of the classical approach, yet, later on, proved to be fully compatible with open economy extensions of Keynesian macroeconomic models.

Many empirical studies subsequently sought to estimate demand elasticities based on this approach to the trade balance. Early studies suggested elasticities were low in the short run which generated 'elasticity pessimism' about trade account adjustment.[1] Later studies also estimated a low response of trade flows in the first year after an exchange rate change, although over longer periods estimates for industrial countries show the Marshall–Lerner condition was usually satisfied.[2]

The evidence that short run export and import demand elasticities are low also provides a justification for the so-called J curve phenomenon, which suggests that after a devaluation or depreciation, a pre-existing trade deficit initially widens before eventually narrowing. J curves are also often explained with reference to contracts.[3] For instance, soon after a devaluation, recorded export and import volumes may for some months simply reflect purchasing decisions based on the old exchange rate, so that the devaluation only raises the value of recorded imports, whereas exports measured in domestic currency do not change. Moreover, sluggish trade account adjustment to changes in competitiveness may reflect lags in producing additional exports, although acknowledging supply constraints on the export side contravenes one of the assumptions underlying the Marshall–Lerner condition.

3.4 THE DEPENDENT ECONOMY APPROACH

The elasticities approach to the external accounts with its sole emphasis on the effects of relative price changes on the trade account, to the neglect of other macroeconomic influences, obviously seemed incomplete by the 1950s, by which time Keynes' *General Theory of Employment, Interest and Money* (1936) had profoundly influenced macroeconomic thinking. On the issue of external account determination, *The General Theory* was silent. Indeed, this profoundly influential book could be criticised for leading modern macroeconomics astray insofar as it reasoned on the assumption of a closed economy, a line of enquiry at odds with the emphasis on international linkages in the writings of the other great English economists including David Ricardo, John Stuart Mill and Alfred Marshall.

It was left to another English economist James Meade (1952) to cast balance of payments analysis in an explicit macroeconomic framework which made sense under the rules governing the Bretton Woods system. Using a framework which was in many ways a precursor to the Mundell–Fleming approach to be discussed shortly, Meade allowed for some capital mobility in his analysis of the external accounts and was first to draw the distinction between the often conflicting goals of internal balance (full employment) and external balance (balance of payments stability). At the same time, Alexander (1952) working at the International Monetary Fund, highlighted the distinction between national product and national expenditure or absorption as earlier discussed in Chapter 2 and expressed in equation (1.1).

Alexander's absorption approach provided a crucial insight by stressing the importance of analysing the external accounts in the context of overall spending and production in contrast to the strictly partial nature of the elasticities approach. Alexander (1959) later attempted a synthesis of the elasticities and absorption approaches. However, this was disappointing as it did not simultaneously consider the interaction of relative price and income effects.

3.4.1 The Basic Model

An absorption related approach which did successfully model the contemporaneous effects of changing relative prices and expenditure was proposed by Swan (1960) and Salter (1959). What distinguished this approach was a markedly different specification of goods markets for small open economies. Previous macroeconomic approaches had often assumed implicitly that all goods were exportable and that the prices of goods produced domestically were endogenous, whereas the prices of imports in foreign exchange were exogenous.

In contrast, the Swan-Salter approach highlighted the goods market dichotomy between tradables and non-tradables.[4] According to Swan, the prices a small economy receives for exports and pays for imports '... are independent of domestic conditions of supply and demand' (1960, p.53) whereas Salter (1959) termed non-tradables as goods '...which do not enter into world trade; their prices are determined solely by internal costs and demand' (p.226).

Also known as the 'dependent economy' or Australian model, this approach assumes a given terms of trade, here measured by the ratio of the exogenously determined prices received for exportables to the exogenously determined prices paid for importables. With this assumption, exportables and importables can be lumped together as tradables by virtue of Hicks (1946) composite commodity theorem: 'A collection of physical things can always be treated as if they were identical in the units of a simple commodity so long as their relative prices can be assumed unchanged ...' (p.33). Hence tradables consist of exports, imports, export substitutes and import competing goods, whereas non-tradables are usually imagined as the bulk of services or goods prevented from entering into world trade because of prohibitive transport costs or tariffs.

The centrally managed nominal exchange rate converts the given world prices of tradables into domestic currency terms ($P_T = eP_T^*$) and the real exchange rate (V), or competitiveness is here defined as the ratio of the domestic price of non-tradables (P_N) to the price of tradables (P_T):

$$V \equiv \frac{P_N}{P_T} .$$

In the dependent economy model, external balance is synonymous with a balanced trade account and capital flows are absent. Moreover, without servicing costs on earlier capital flows, the current account equates with the trade account, ignoring other international transfers. Internal balance is the correspondence between the output of, and expenditure on, non-tradables. The Salter diagram below (Figure 3.1) depicts the simultaneous attainment of internal and external balance at point E.

The production transformation curve indicates possible output combinations for existing technology and factor endowments. For a given set of production possibilities, a rise in tradable output requires forgone non-tradable output. On the other hand, the community in-difference curve represents ex ante absorption in Alexander's sense.

With reference to Figure 3.1, full equilibrium implies OT tradables are supplied and demanded at the given real exchange rate ensuring external balance, whereas ON non-tradables are supplied and demanded at the same real exchange rate ensuring internal balance. The approach suggests that departures from internal or external imbalance may occur if competitiveness changes or a disparity arises between output and expenditure. In such circumstances, a policy response simultaneously combining managed exchange rate changes and changes in autonomous expenditure becomes necessary. There are two instruments for two targets consistent with Tinbergen's (1952) rule.

For given technology and factor endowments, the supply side of the model may be expressed in symbols as $Y_{T,N} = Y_{T,N}(V)$. The expenditure side is $A_{T,N} = A_{T,N}(V, \bar{A})$ where $\bar{A}$ is the autonomous component of expenditure which can be influenced by fiscal or monetary policy.

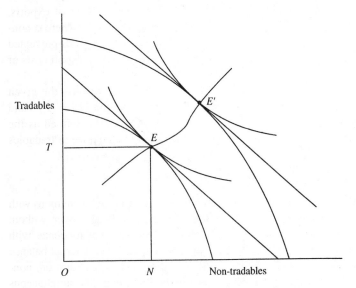

Figure 3.1   The dependent economy model

Hence, production of tradables and non-tradables is in the short run, simply a function of competitiveness, yet absorption is a function of both competitiveness and autonomous expenditure.

Internal balance obtains when $Y_N(V) = A_N(V,A)$ and external balance obtains when $Y_T(V) = A_T(V,A)$. Differentiating these equations totally then allows us to derive the internal and external balance loci. Starting with the internal balance locus (*NN*)

$$\frac{\partial Y_N}{\partial V} dV = \frac{\partial A_N}{\partial V} dV + \frac{\partial A_N}{\partial \bar{A}} d\bar{A}.$$

$$\therefore \frac{dV}{d\bar{A}} = \frac{\partial A_N}{\partial \bar{A}} \Big/ \left(\frac{\partial Y_N}{\partial V} - \frac{\partial A_N}{\partial V} \right) > 0.$$

For the external balance locus (*TT*)

$$\frac{\partial Y_T}{\partial V} dV = \frac{\partial A_T}{\partial V} dV + \frac{\partial A_T}{\partial \bar{A}} d\bar{A}.$$

$$\therefore \frac{dV}{d\bar{A}} = \frac{\partial A_T}{\partial \bar{A}} \Big/ \left(\frac{\partial Y_T}{\partial V} - \frac{\partial A_T}{\partial V} \right) < 0.$$

Depicting these loci in $V - \bar{A}$ space yields the Swan diagram (Figure 3.2) with its four 'zones of economic unhappiness'.

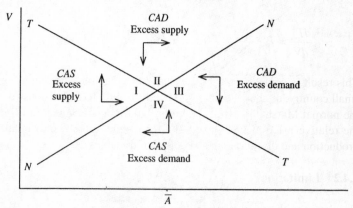

Figure 3.2   The Swan diagram

Intuitively, the internal balance schedule slopes upward because as competitiveness worsens (a rise in V), net exports fall, and autonomous expenditure must increase to compensate for this. The external balance schedule slopes downward because an increase in autonomous expenditure worsens net exports unless offset by an improvement in competitiveness (a fall in V).

Above the NN locus the economy has underutilised resources, below it there are excess demand pressures. Above the TT line the economy experiences a trade (current) account deficit, below it a trade account surplus.

An economy out of equilibrium reaches simultaneous internal and external balance through the combined use of managed exchange rate changes to alter competitiveness and activist fiscal and monetary policy to raise or lower total expenditure. For instance, an economy experiencing excess aggregate demand pressures and an external deficit (zone III) could restore internal balance by contractionary policy and restore external balance by devaluing the exchange rate.

Given its particular goods market specification, devaluation improves the trade balance and revaluation worsens the trade balance unambiguously. Totally differentiating the expression for the trade balance in foreign exchange terms, $T^* = (Y_T(V) - A_T(V))P_T^*$ with respect to V, where Y_T and A_T are volumes, yields

$$dT^* = P_T^* \frac{\partial Y_T}{\partial V} dV - P_T^* \frac{\partial A_T}{\partial V} dV.$$

$$\therefore \quad \frac{dT^*}{dV} = P_T^* \left(\frac{\partial Y_T}{\partial V} - \frac{\partial A_T}{\partial V} \right) < 0.$$

This result is compatible with the elasticities condition pertaining to a small country, as shown earlier, but contrasts with the conditionality of the normal Marshall–Lerner condition. Intuitively, devaluation lowers the relative price of non-traded goods to traded goods, encouraging production and discouraging absorption of tradables.

3.4.2 Limitations

Consistent with the international economic environment of the 1950s and 1960s, the original dependent economy model assumed the exchange rate was managed and ignored external capital flows and the possibility that domestic saving and investment could diverge. Once the exchange rate is permitted to float however, external balance is automatically achieved in the model as exports must always equal imports as an equilibrium condition in the foreign exchange market. Hence, a dependent economy always finds itself on the *TT* locus of the Swan diagram and the goal of external balance becomes redundant. Unfortunately, the model cannot be so easily adapted to allow for international capital mobility, a factor which severely limits the model's usefulness as a framework for analysing external account determination in the 1990s.

3.5 MONETARY APPROACHES

The developments in international macroeconomics and balance of payments theory from the elasticities approach, which first emerged in the 1920s, to the absorption related approaches of the 1950s and 1960s mainly emphasised adjustment in the goods markets with the trade balance providing the measure of external disequilibrium. However, a different approach to the external accounts reemphasising the role of money in the external adjustment process emerged in the literature by the late 1960s and 1970s, although an earlier version of the approach had been proposed by Polak (1957), another International Monetary Fund economist (see also IMF (1977)). This approach became known as the monetary approach to the balance of payments (MABP).[5]

The MABP had more in common with the original Humean approach than other subsequent macroeconomic approaches because it restored the notion that the external adjustment process was essentially self-equilibrating and not of itself a concern. Moreover, like the classical approach, it afforded the demand and supply of money balances a central role. Other Humean features of this approach were that growth in national income was exogenously determined by real factors such as advances in technology and population growth and that demands for particular national currencies by domestic residents were stable functions of a few variables, the most important being real income. Unlike the original price–specie–flow mechanism however, changes in relative export and import prices on which the elasticities approach focussed were eliminated from the analysis.

Instead of examining the trade or current account imbalance per se, the MABP shifted attention to the overall balance of payments as a monetary phenomenon reflecting the change in the central banks reserve holdings. With reference to our real and financial flows matrix of Chapter 2 (Table 2.1), the analysis centred on the relationships between the money base and changes in foreign currency reserves (rows two and seven), with the central bank (column five) playing a prominent role.

Another distinguishing feature of the MABP was its emphasis on stocks, in contrast to the earlier flow-oriented approaches. It stressed that the flow of international reserves, as the measure of external imbalance under fixed rates, essentially reflected domestic money market disequilibrium which could only be restored when the stock demand and stock supply of real balances reached their desired levels.

3.5.1 The Basic Model

The monetary approach actually encompasses a wide class of models. For instance, one version of the monetary approach proposed by Dornbusch (1973) assumes a small open economy facing world prices for all goods produced and consumed, but there is no capital account. This version also invokes the output–absorption distinction. The main features of the approach are now outlined below.

The demand for (L) money is considered a stable function of income such that

$$L = kP\overline{Y} \tag{3.28}$$

where k is a parameter, P is the domestic price level and $\overline{Y}$ is constant real output at the level of full employment.

If money, simply defined as money base, is the only asset, then the difference between output and expenditure, the trade imbalance, must be equal to the change in the money base held by the public.

$$dM^s = P\overline{Y} - A. \tag{3.29}$$

Furthermore, under fixed rates,

$$dR = dM^s. \tag{3.30}$$

The difference between absorption and income is also related to the difference between actual and desired money holdings,

$$P\overline{Y} - A = \alpha (L - M^s)$$

$0 < \alpha < 1$, where α is an adjustment parameter. From (3.28), (3.29) and (3.30) we can write

$$dR = \alpha (kP\overline{Y} - M^s). \tag{3.31}$$

Equation (3.31) expresses the self-correcting nature of any discrepancy between money supply and money demand. For instance, if money demand exceeds the available supply, dR will be positive, indicating that a balance-of-payments surplus will eventuate and persist until it raises the money supply to the level consistent with desired money holdings. On the contrary, if the domestic supply of money available to be held by residents exceeds the level desired, there will be a balance of payments deficit which will only last until desired and actual money stocks are again equal. Graphically, the model can be illustrated by a simple phase diagram (Figure 3.3) which shows the adjustment mechanism is stable.

If for instance the money supply is M_1^s which falls short of desired cash holdings at $kP\overline{Y}$, then there would be reduced absorption (or

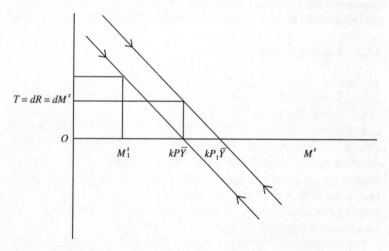

Figure 3.3   The monetary approach to the balance of payments

hoarding) by domestic residents in an attempt to accumulate cash balances. This would manifest as a trade surplus matched by a rise in reserves. A steady expansion of the domestic money supply continues until desired and actual money stocks again coincide. At that point external balance is restored.

Several important policy implications followed from the MABP. First, the approach stressed, as did Hume, that under fixed rates the money supply is in the long run endogenous, determined not by the central bank but essentially by the public's demand for cash balances. Furthermore, devaluations will only have a transitory effect on the balance of payments and only to the extent that they affect stock equilibrium in the money market.[6] This is also shown in the figure above. By invoking the absolute purchasing power parity condition ($P = eP^*$) devaluation firstly raises the domestic price level to P_1. Domestic residents again attempt to restore real cash balances to the previous level by reducing absorption. In so doing, a balance-of-payments surplus arises and persists until the nominal money supply increases (proportionate to the increase in the price level) to restore money stock equilibrium.

Note that the nature of the mechanism transmitting the change in the exchange rate to the balance on the external account is altogether different from the elasticities approach. Indeed, advocates of the MABP considered the elasticities conditions irrelevant since all prices inevitably rose in the devaluing country to the extent of the devaluation itself.

3.5.2 Limitations and Extensions

The MABP was in many respects a restatement of the original classical approach. Similarly, it is subject to criticism about its implicit assumption of free and flexible labour and goods markets. With the generalised move to floating rates in the 1970s, the MABP became somewhat redundant as a means of understanding the external accounts; with floating exchange rates, the overall balance of payments as a measure of a central bank's support for a particular exchange rate ceased to be the constraint it had been hitherto under the Bretton Woods system. Accordingly, attention shifted to the determinants of the exchange rate as the macroeconomic variable reflecting the pressure of external adjustment.

The essential ingredients of the MABP were then deployed to model exchange rate determination with continued emphasis on the role played by relative money demands and supplies. The monetary or asset approach to the exchange rate generated a vast theoretical and empirical literature,[7] a survey of which is not relevant here since the external accounts subsequently slipped from view. Implicitly, however, these models accepted that the traditional notion of external imbalance as a quantity constraint no longer mattered for policy purposes.

Relatedly, the portfolio balance (PB) approach to the open economy developed from the 1960s and included domestic and foreign bonds in addition to money.[8] It extended earlier work on general portfolio theory advanced by Markowitz (1952) and Tobin (1958).

The PB approach usually suggests capital flows are short lived phenomena which cease once desired and actual financial asset holdings equate. Financial capital is not perfectly mobile by assumption, though alternative financial assets remain gross substitutes in demand. By restricting attention to nominal financial wealth held by domestic residents and by using total financial wealth as a scale variable in asset demand equations, the PB approach has been used to explain the short run comparative static effects of changes in the domestic supply of money and bonds on the nominal exchange rate and domestic interest rate.

Within the PB class of open economy models, some authors have recognized a role for the current account in terms of its implications for the international investment position and hence for financial wealth holdings. For example, some authors have explicitly modelled the feedback effects of current account imbalances on the exchange rate.[9] However, the emphasis in these models is on financial phenomena to the neglect of real phenomena. In any case, open economy PB models ultimately seek to explain exchange rate and domestic interest rate determination, as opposed to external account determination as such, which is the major focus of this book.

3.6   THE MUNDELL–FLEMING APPROACH

Perhaps the most influential and easily the most elaborate macro-economic model of an economy transacting with the rest of the world is the Mundell–Fleming (MF) model, first proposed by Fleming (1962) and Mundell (1963).[10] Essentially, the model is the open economy extension of the Keynesian IS–LM framework (following Hicks

(1937)) linking international financial capital flows, interest differentials, exchange rates, competitiveness, exports, imports and national income.

What distinguishes the MF model is the prominence afforded international financial capital flows in the process of national income determination. It shifts attention away from the current account, to the overall balance of payments under managed exchange rates and to the exchange rate itself as the key external adjustment variable under floating exchange rates.

MF analysis has been highly influential mainly because of its conclusions about the effectiveness of monetary and fiscal policy for income stabilization purposes under alternative exchange rate regimes. In the following exposition, although the policy implications of adopting fixed versus floating exchange rates are addressed, discussion centres mainly on the floating exchange rate version with internationally mobile financial flows since those are the conditions most relevant to many industrial nations in current circumstances. The major predictions of the approach are first derived mathematically and then exposited diagrammatically with particular reference to the significance of capital movements, as defined by the approach, and how they affect the current account.

3.6.1 The Basic Model

In its basic version, MF assumes a small open economy with a perfectly elastic aggregate supply curve, static exchange rate expectations and perfect capital mobility. On the real side of the economy, the model assumes unemployed resources and a fixed price level. On the financial side there are only three financial assets (rows two, four and seven of Table 2.1): domestic base money which is non-substitutable for foreign base money, domestic and foreign bonds which are perfectly substitutable for each other and foreign reserves (used to manage the exchange rate in the fixed exchange rate version of the model).

Since static exchange rate expectations mean that the exchange rate is not expected to deviate from its present level, the assumption of perfect capital mobility implies that home and foreign interest rates (r and r^* respectively) will always be equal, both in nominal and real terms, since there is no inflation.

Consistent with its Keynesian underpinnings, gross domestic product is demand determined. Part of total absorption is autonomous, while the rest depends negatively on the domestic interest rate, particularly through domestic private investment, and positively on national income, through the propensity of households to consume. Government expenditure may be either public consumption or public investment and is included within the autonomous component of total spending along with private autonomous consumption and investment. Net exports (or the current account in the absence of net income or transfers paid abroad) are a function of the domestic propensity to import and the exchange rate. Given the fixed price level assumption, nominal exchange rate changes translate one for one to real exchange rate changes since the real exchange rate is defined as $\dfrac{eP^*}{P}$. The Marshall–Lerner condition derived above is assumed to hold.

Equilibrium in the money market is given by the stock equality of real money demand (L), which depends negatively on the domestic interest rate and positively on real income, and the real money supply, (M^s).

3.6.2 Comparative Statics

This section now mathematically examines the comparative statics of the MF model under floating exchange rates with varying degrees of capital mobility.[11]

Goods market equilibrium may be written as the condition that total injections equal leakages.

$$\overline{A} + I(r) + X(e) = S(Y) + M(Y, e) \tag{3.32}$$

where $I_r < 0, X_e > 0, 0 < S_y < 1, 0 < M_y < 1, M_e < 0$.

$\overline{A}$ denotes total autonomous expenditure including private and public consumption and private and public investment expenditure; the other variables are as defined above and in Chapter 2.

Money market equilibrium is given by the stock equality of real money demand and the real money supply.

$$M^s = L(Y, r) \tag{3.33}$$

$$L_y > 0, \quad L_r < 0.$$

The external accounts under a floating exchange rate can also be expressed as

$$B = X(e) - M(Y,e) + KAB(r) = 0. \tag{3.34}$$

Total differentiation of equations (3.32), (3.33) and (3.34) yields, after some rearrangement, the following matrix:

$$\begin{bmatrix} S_y + M_y & -I_r & (M_e - X_e) \\ L_y & L_r & 0 \\ M_y & -KAB_r & (M_e - X_e) \end{bmatrix} \begin{bmatrix} dY \\ dr \\ de \end{bmatrix} = \begin{bmatrix} d\bar{A} \\ dM^s \\ 0 \end{bmatrix}$$

The coefficient matrix may be inverted to yield

$$\begin{bmatrix} dY \\ dr \\ de \end{bmatrix} = \begin{bmatrix} \dfrac{L_r(M_e - X_e)}{D} & \dfrac{(I_r - KAB_r)(M_e - X_e)}{D} & \dfrac{-L_r(M_e - X_e)}{D} \\ \dfrac{-L_y(M_e - X_e)}{D} & \dfrac{S_y(M_e - X_e)}{D} & \dfrac{L_y(M_e - X_e)}{D} \\ \dfrac{-(L_y KAB_r + L_r M_y)}{D} & \dfrac{KAB_r(S_y + M_y) - I_r M_y}{D} & \dfrac{-L_r(S_y + M_y) + L_y I_r}{D} \end{bmatrix} \begin{bmatrix} d\bar{A} \\ dM^s \\ 0 \end{bmatrix}$$

where the determinant of the coefficient matrix,

$$D = (M_e - X_e)(L_r S_y - L_y KAB_r + I_r L_y) > 0.$$

a)   Increased autonomous expenditure.

It follows that the multipliers for a change in autonomous expenditure are

$$\frac{dY}{d\bar{A}} = \frac{L_r}{L_r S_y - L_y KAB_r + I_r L_y} > 0$$

$$\frac{dr}{d\bar{A}} = \frac{-L_y}{L_r S_y - L_y KAB_r + I_r L_y} > 0$$

$$\frac{de}{d\bar{A}} = \frac{-(L_y KAB_r + L_r M_y)}{(M_e - X_e)(L_r S_y - L_y KAB_r + I_r L_y)} \gtrless 0.$$

This is ambiguous since $L_y KAB_r$ is positive and $L_r M_y$ is negative.

The above results suggest that an increase in autonomous expenditure, including increased public spending due to discretionary fiscal expansion, raises both the equilibrium level of income and interest rate. The effect on the exchange rate is ambiguous. If financial capital flows are perfectly mobile in the MF sense, $KAB_r \to \infty$. Hence, the above multipliers under floating exchange rates reduce to

$$\frac{dY}{d\overline{A}} = 0$$

$$\frac{dr}{d\overline{A}} = 0$$

$$\frac{de}{d\overline{A}} = \frac{1}{M_e - X_e} < 0.$$

Therefore, under floating exchange rates, increased autonomous expenditure is ineffective in raising national income but appreciates the exchange rate.

Alternatively, if financial capital is completely immobile, $KAB_r = 0$, and the multipliers reduce to

$$\frac{dY}{d\overline{A}} = \frac{L_r}{L_r S_y + I_r L_y} > 0$$

$$\frac{dr}{d\overline{A}} = \frac{-L_y}{L_r S_y + I_r L_y} > 0$$

$$\frac{de}{d\overline{A}} = \frac{-L_r M_y}{(M_e - X_e)(L_r S_y + I_r L_y)} > 0.$$

Modifying the perfect capital mobility assumption therefore allows autonomous expenditure increases to impact positively on income and the domestic interest rate.

b) Monetary expansion.

From the matrix, the multipliers from a monetary expansion reduce to

$$\frac{dY}{dM^s} = \frac{I_r - KAB_r}{L_rS_y - L_yKAB_r + I_rL_y} > 0$$

$$\frac{dr}{dM^s} = \frac{S_y}{L_rS_y - L_yKAB_r + I_rL_y} < 0$$

$$\frac{de}{dM^s} = \frac{KAB_r(S_y + M_y) - I_rM_y}{(M_e - X_e)(L_rS_y - L_yKAB_r + I_rL_y)} > 0.$$

Hence expansionary monetary policy raises equilibrium income, lowers the domestic interest rate and depreciates the exchange rate.

With perfect capital mobility, $KAB_r \rightarrow \infty$, the multipliers are

$$\frac{dY}{dM^s} = \frac{1}{L_y} > 0$$

$$\frac{dr}{dM^s} = 0$$

$$\frac{de}{dM^s} = \frac{S_y + M_y}{-(M_e - X_e)L_y} > 0.$$

This suggests that monetary policy is effective in raising income and depreciating the exchange rate, but that perfect capital mobility ensures the domestic interest rate does not change.

Again varying the capital mobility assumption, if $KAB_r = 0$, the multipliers reduce to

$$\frac{dY}{dM^s} = \frac{I_r}{L_rS_y + I_rL_y} > 0$$

$$\frac{dr}{dM^s} = \frac{S_y}{L_rS_y + I_rL_y} < 0$$

$$\frac{de}{dM^s} = \frac{-I_rM_y}{(M_e - X_e)(L_rS_y + I_rL_y)} > 0.$$

Under these conditions, monetary expansion raises equilibrium income, lowers the domestic interest rate and depreciates the exchange rate.

c) Stability analysis.

Stability analysis concerns the time paths of variables when the economy is out of equilibrium. To conduct stability analysis it is therefore necessary to make assumptions about how the key variables in the MF model behave when away from their equilibrium values. Accordingly, the above version of the MF model may be expressed in dynamic terms as

$$\frac{dY}{dt} = \alpha_1[\bar{A} + I(r) + X(e) - S(Y) - M(Y,e)] \tag{3.35}$$

$$\frac{dr}{dt} = \alpha_2[L(Y,r) - M^s] \tag{3.36}$$

$$\frac{de}{dt} = -\alpha_3[X(e) - M(Y,e) + KAB(r)]. \tag{3.37}$$

Equation (3.35) suggests that income adjustment is proportional to the gap between injections (autonomous expenditure, interest sensitive investment and exports) and leakages (saving and imports). The speed of adjustment is determined by reaction coefficient α_1.

Equation (3.36) implies that if real money demand rises above the real money supply then the interest rate rises at a rate determined by reaction coefficient α_2.

Equation (3.37) states that the exchange rate appreciates at a speed governed by reaction coefficient α_3 as capital inflow exceeds net exports. The above implicit functions can be replaced with linear approximations in the neighbourhood of equilibrium, such that the equations may be rewritten in linear homogeneous form as

$$\frac{dY}{dt} = \alpha_1[-(S_y + M_y)(Y - \bar{Y}) + I_r(r - \bar{r}) + (M_e - X_e)(e - \bar{e})]$$

$$\frac{dr}{dt} = \alpha_2[L_y(Y - \bar{Y}) + L_r(r - \bar{r})]$$

$$\frac{de}{dt} = -\alpha_3[-M_y(Y - \overline{Y}) + KAB_r(r - \overline{r}) - (M_e - X_e)(e - \overline{e})]$$

where $\overline{Y}, \overline{r}, \overline{e}$ denote final equilibrium values.

Solutions to these differential equations must express the values of the variables as functions of time and be of the form

$$Y = \overline{Y} + \beta_1 E^{qt} \tag{3.38}$$

$$r = \overline{r} + \beta_2 E^{qt} \tag{3.39}$$

$$e = \overline{e} + \beta_3 E^{qt} \tag{3.40}$$

where E is the exponential. If Y, r and e approach their equilibrium values $\overline{Y}, \overline{r}, \overline{e}$, the system is stable and for this to occur the term q (the characteristic root) must be negative for the dynamic component of the right-hand expression to approach zero through time. Differentiating equations (3.38), (3.39) and (3.40) with respect to time yields

$$\frac{dY}{dt} = q\beta_1 E^{qt} = q(Y - \overline{Y})$$

$$\frac{dr}{dt} = q\beta_2 E^{qt} = q(r - \overline{r})$$

$$\frac{de}{dt} = q\beta_3 E^{qt} = q(e - \overline{e}).$$

Substituting $q(Y - \overline{Y})$, $q(r - \overline{r})$ and $q(e - \overline{e})$ for $\frac{dY}{dt}, \frac{dr}{dt}$ and $\frac{de}{dt}$ respectively yields the matrix equation:

$$\begin{bmatrix} q + \alpha_1(S_y + M_y) & -\alpha_1 I_r & \alpha_1(M_e - X_e) \\ -\alpha_2 L_y & q - \alpha_2 L_r & 0 \\ -\alpha_3 M_y & \alpha_3 KAB_r & q - \alpha_3(M_e - X_e) \end{bmatrix} \begin{bmatrix} Y - \overline{Y} \\ r - \overline{r} \\ e - \overline{e} \end{bmatrix} = 0$$

The characteristic matrix cannot have an inverse, otherwise displacements from equilibrium would be zero. The characteristic equation derived from the characteristic determinant is

$$q^2 + [\alpha_1(S_y + M_y) - \alpha_2 L_r + \alpha_3(M_e - X_e)]q^2 + [-\alpha_1\alpha_2 L_r(S_y + M_y) - \alpha_1\alpha_3(S_y + M_y)$$

$$(M_e - X_e) + \alpha_2\alpha_3 L_r(M_e - X_e)] + \alpha_1\alpha_2\alpha_3(M_e - X_e)(L_r S_y - L_y KAB_r + I_r L_y) = 0.$$

All coefficients must be positive for stability to obtain. Since S_y, M_y and I_r are positive and L_r and I_r are negative, this condition is met provided that exchange depreciation reduces net imports (that is, $M_e - X_e < 0$) in accordance with the Marshall–Lerner condition.

3.6.3 Diagrammatic Analysis

The standard effectiveness results set out above are usually derived graphically using the familiar *IS –LM –BP* framework. Shown below is the conventional presentation, augmented by a supplementary framework, based on the same Keynesian assumptions, which allows us to trace more explicitly the effects of autonomous expenditure and monetary shocks on the trade account, as well as the saving-investment imbalance.

Consider first the implications of an autonomous spending increase on the trade account under the assumptions of a floating exchange rate and perfect capital mobility. In terms of *IS–LM–BP* analysis, the *IS* curve moves to the right, putting upward pressure on the domestic interest rate. However, this incipient interest rate rise attracts foreign capital, appreciating the currency. Hence, the exchange rate is assumed to be entirely capital account driven. The loss of competitiveness thereby crowds out net exports shifting back the *IS* curve to its initial position.

Accompanying the *IS–LM–BP* diagram is what we will term an *NS–NX* framework. This supplementary framework highlights the effects of various shocks on the economy's saving-investment and external account imbalances which, as demonstrated in Chapter 2, must be equal to each other ex post. In full equilibrium the saving-investment and external account imbalances must of course also be equal ex ante. The upward-sloping *NS* schedule shows net saving and is drawn for given autonomous expenditure and domestic interest rate. An increase in income raises net saving as the marginal propensity to consume is less than unity and investment is autonomous. Hence the slope of this schedule is determined by the marginal propensity to save which lies between zero and unity. The downward-sloping *NX* schedule is drawn for a given level of autonomous exports and competitiveness. This schedule shows that as income rises, imports increase and hence the trade deficit widens. Its slope is minus the marginal propensity to import. An improvement in competitiveness shifts the net export schedule to the right as the Marshall–Lerner condition is satisfied. For ease of exposition of the comparative static effects on the trade account

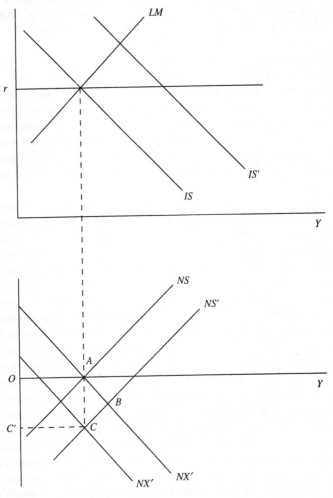

Figure 3.4   Domestic expenditure shocks in the MF model with perfect capital mobility

and saving–investment imbalance, it is assumed that in initial equilibrium the trade account is balanced.

Consider first an increase in autonomous expenditure as shown above in Figure 3.4. This shifts the *IS* curve to the right and also shifts the net saving (*NS*) schedule rightward from point *A* to *B*, raising the trade deficit through increased imports. However, as competitiveness worsens because capital inflow appreciates the exchange rate, the *NX* schedule shifts left such that the trade deficit increases by *OC'*. However, there is no net effect on income.

On the contrary, a monetary expansion under these assumptions has a powerful effect on national income. A rightward shift of the *LM* curve tends to lower interest rates, which, given the perfect capital mobility assumption, depreciates the exchange rate. This improves competitiveness and shifts the *IS* curve to the right. In the *NS–NX* framework, the incipient lower interest rate has no effect on autonomous expenditure but only depreciates the exchange rate which shifts the *NX* schedule. In this case, the trade deficit unambiguously improves, as shown in Figure 3.5.

Domestic expenditure and monetary shocks have quite different effects if capital is assumed immobile compared with the perfect capital mobility assumption, as earlier shown mathematically. Again with reference to the standard *IS–LM–BP* diagram, the effects of various shocks on the interest rate, exchange rate, income and the trade account can be modelled by varying the slope of the *BP* curve. For illustrative purposes, consider the effect of capital immobility ($KAB_r = 0$) in the limiting case of a vertical *BP* curve (Figure 3.6), showing that capital flows are completely unresponsive to interest rate changes, as may occur for example for economies with prohibitive exchange controls. In such circumstances, the external accounts only comprise a trade account in common with earlier approaches. If the exchange rate floats, the trade balance will always be balanced through changes in the exchange rate itself. If the exchange rate is fixed, the trade deficit becomes the balance of payments deficit and would usually be financed by a rundown in the central bank's official reserves.

Increased autonomous expenditure under floating rates shifts the *IS* curve to the right, raising the trade deficit, and *NS* also shifts. However, with immobile capital the exchange rate depreciates to restore a balanced trade account, thus further shifting the *IS* curve as well as the *BP* and *NX* curves.

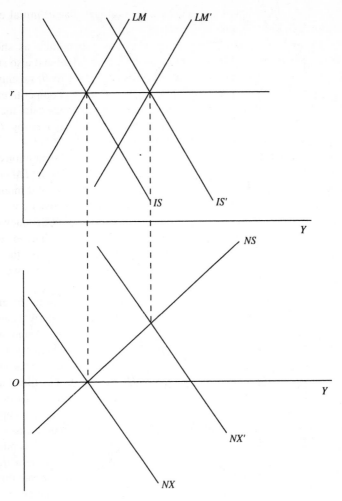

Figure 3.5   Monetary expansion in the MF model
with perfect capital mobility

Finally, a money supply increase under the same assumptions
worsens the trade balance as income and imports rise. This depreciates
the currency and thereby further shifts the *IS* curve to the right. The *BP*
and *NX* curves also shift to the right, as shown in Figure 3.7.

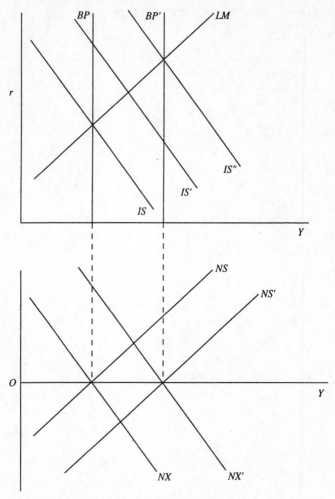

Figure 3.6   Domestic expenditure shocks in the MF model
with capital immobility

The basic MF model may also be used to provide a theoretical rationale for linking expansionary fiscal policy, as manifested in wider budget deficits, to trade or current account deficits. This causal link, termed the 'twin deficits' hypothesis, is a specific case of the more general case which treats the comparative static effects of increased

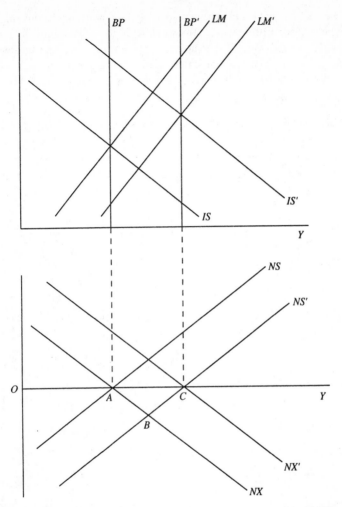

Figure 3.7   Monetary expansion in the MF model with capital immobility

domestic expenditure under floating exchange rates with capital mobility, as outlined in Figure 3.5 above.

Budget deficits may widen as either public consumption or public investment expenditure increases or because income taxes are cut. Public expenditure increases directly augment autonomous expenditure whereas tax cuts are assumed to stimulate household consumption expenditure. Either way, consistent with the MF approach, bigger budget deficits initially put upward pressure on the domestic interest rate which induces capital inflow. This then appreciates the nominal exchange rate, crowds out net exports and widens the *CAD*. The

Table 3.1   Expenditure and money supply increases under floating and fixed exchange rate regimes

	Floating exchange rate, $KAB_r \to \infty$	*Floating exchange rate,* $KAB_r = 0$	*Fixed exchange rate,* $KAB_r \to \infty$	*Fixed exchange rate,* $KAB_r = 0$
Expenditure increase	$\dfrac{dr}{d\bar{A}} = 0$	$\dfrac{dr}{d\bar{A}} > 0$	$\dfrac{dr}{d\bar{A}} = 0$	$\dfrac{dr}{d\bar{A}} > 0$
	$\dfrac{dY}{d\bar{A}} = 0$	$\dfrac{dY}{d\bar{A}} > 0$	$\dfrac{dY}{d\bar{A}} > 0$	$\dfrac{dY}{d\bar{A}} = 0$
	$\dfrac{de}{d\bar{A}} < 0$	$\dfrac{de}{d\bar{A}} > 0$	$\dfrac{de}{d\bar{A}} = 0$	$\dfrac{de}{d\bar{A}} = 0$
	$\dfrac{dT}{d\bar{A}} < 0$	$\dfrac{dT}{d\bar{A}} = 0$	$\dfrac{dT}{d\bar{A}} < 0$	$\dfrac{dT}{d\bar{A}} = 0$
Money supply increase	$\dfrac{dr}{dM^s} = 0$	$\dfrac{dr}{dM^s} < 0$	$\dfrac{dr}{dM^s} = 0$	$\dfrac{dr}{dM^s} = 0$
	$\dfrac{dY}{dM^s} > 0$	$\dfrac{dY}{dM^s} > 0$	$\dfrac{dY}{dM^s} = 0$	$\dfrac{dY}{dM^s} = 0$
	$\dfrac{de}{dM^s} > 0$	$\dfrac{de}{dM^s} > 0$	$\dfrac{de}{dM^s} = 0$	$\dfrac{de}{dM^s} = 0$
	$\dfrac{dT}{dM^s} > 0$	$\dfrac{dT}{dM^s} = 0$	$\dfrac{dT}{dM^s} = 0$	$\dfrac{dT}{dM^s} = 0$

theoretical limitations of this variant of the MF approach are addressed again in Chapter 5.

Although the augmented *IS–LM–BP* framework has been used to examine the comparative statics of expenditure and monetary shocks under a floating exchange rate with polar degrees of capital mobility, it is also possible to adapt the approach for a fixed rate environment. A summary of the main results under both regimes is included in Table 3.1.

3.6.4 Limitations and Extensions

There are a number of problems with the MF specifications of both the real and financial sides of the economy. Taken together these short-comings and inconsistencies limit its usefulness as a vehicle for understanding the nature and significance of external account determination, notwithstanding its popularity as the ruling textbook framework for interpreting international macroeconomic policy issues. These limitations can be traced to the underlying assumptions of the basic MF model, many of which have hitherto only been addressed piecemeal in the open economy literature.

Goods Market Specification

Starting with the goods side, the heart of traditional Keynesian analysis, the model implicitly assumes all goods are internationally tradable and the economy is small. However, domestic producers and consumers are not price takers in the dependent economy sense which is somewhat unrealistic for many small economies, such as Australia, where in fact many goods, particularly tradable commodities, are highly substitutable for foreign goods. In contrast, the model asymmetrically specifies that in financial markets, domestic and foreign bonds may be perfect substitutes under the perfect capital mobility assumption, ignoring the possibility of international interest risk premia.

Moreover, the standard MF assumption that exports are autonomous with respect to national income does not allow exports to be negatively related to absorption, $\left(\dfrac{\partial X}{\partial A} < 0 \right)$ as implied by the dependent economy approach.

The autonomous exports assumption seems implausible since increased domestic expenditure not only means more spending by households, firms and government on goods produced abroad, showing up as higher imports, but should also mean increased spending on goods produced at home, including goods otherwise destined for sale to foreigners. To assume exports are autonomous implies the domestic income elasticity of demand for exportables is zero which seems unlikely.

The simple Keynesian consumption function included in the basic model is of course subject to all the criticisms and alternative speci- fications such as the relative, permanent and life cycle hypotheses expounded in the closed economy literature.[12] Likewise, the closed economy literature contains alternative, more sophisticated investment functions, than that proposed in the standard MF model.[13]

With respect to the impact of government spending and taxing on total expenditure, the MF model implies that activist fiscal policies can be easily implemented, without acknowledging the practical policy complications which arise because of lags due to delays in perceiving changed economic circumstances and to institutional impediments which frustrate speedy implementation of discretionary budgetary changes.

Omission of Output and Price Level Dynamics

Another unrealistic assumption of the basic MF model is that the price level is fixed. This deficiency has however been addressed by some authors[14] who allow exchange rate changes to affect the price level and hence real balances with feedback effects on the real sector, thus modifying but not substantially changing the standard conclusions of the approach. Relatedly, the implicit assumption of the basic MF model that aggregate supply is perfectly elastic has been relaxed. For instance, Bruce and Purvis (1985) demonstrate that the standard policy ineffect- iveness results are still valid only if nominal wages are rigid; otherwise with variable wages and a changing price level there are associated supply side effects which, with perfect capital mobility, can render monetary policy ineffective but make fiscal policy effective under floating rates.[15]

Despite recognizing the need for a supply side and changing price level, these extended MF models continue, however, to constrain the output and expenditure aggregates of the national accounts to the same value, in and out of equilibrium, contrary to the absorption related approaches. Notwithstanding the extensions which have been proposed, the MF approach therefore still basically rests on a simplistic, ad hoc formulation of the external accounts.[16] As expressed in equation (3.34) above, the trade account and capital flows are treated only partially and remain distinct from the rest of the national accounts and flow of funds accounts. The accounting foundations of the MF model are weak and bear little relation to the total national accounting and flow of funds framework of Chapter 2. The flow of funds framework in particular suggests that models of the external accounts should not divorce real and financial flows irrespective of the time period under analysis. In short, the extensive literature spawned by the original MF model does not recognise that real and sectoral financial flows are indeed inseparable, implying that both the current and capital accounts may be determined simultaneously by a common set of economic influences.

Financial Market Specification

A more specific shortcoming of the financial specification of the basic MF model concerns the inconsistency between having a flow equilibrium condition for the capital account, which underlies the *BP* curve, and the stock equilibrium condition in the domestic money market, which underlies the *LM* curve. Indeed, the model expects us to accept that the stock demand and supply of money in the domestic money market is invariant in final equilibrium, yet that simultaneously the net foreign investment position and hence the stock of financial and real wealth are changing, consistent with capital flow equilibrium. The model also neglects the extent to which capital flows may finance domestic investment as well as the possibility that rising external indebtedness consequent upon capital inflows may check the equilibrium capital inflow, should it affect a nation's international creditworthiness.

In treating capital flows simply as purchases and sales of debt instruments, the MF model also omits foreign purchases of equities (row five of Table 2.1) or indeed other real assets such as property which may often account for a significant portion of total capital flows. Foreign claims to real domestic assets may also help explain the process of real international capital transfer as argued in the next chapter.

Turning to the specification of the domestic money market, both the MF, PB and indeed monetary approaches commonly argue that domestic interest rates are determined by the interaction between the stock demand for money and the stock supply of money. This stock perspective on domestic interest rate determination has been questioned by Tsiang (1989), citing Keynes (1937) and Tobin (1982) (both early proponents of the stock approach) in support. Tsiang argues that the loanable funds approach to interest rate determination, a flow perspective, provides a suitable alternative to the traditional stock approach.

The loanable funds approach, earlier advocated by Robertson (1940), but with antecedents in pre-Keynesian theory, asserts that the domestic interest rate is essentially determined at any time by the prevailing supply and demand for loanable funds, in a financial system where funds are endlessly exchanged in a circular flow. Since we are mainly concerned with the determination of external account flows, particularly in the context of an integrated real and financial accounting system, the loanable funds approach, with suitable extension to the open economy, suggests a different perspective on the current and capital accounts. An extended loanable funds approach will be outlined in the next chapter.

The basic MF model also fails to account for exchange rate expectations which are implicitly assumed static. Dornbusch (1976a) addressed this omission by allowing forward looking expectations about the exchange rate to drive a wedge between domestic and foreign interest rates through the uncovered interest parity condition. By allowing asset prices to adjust more quickly than goods prices, Dornbusch's MF foundations emphasise the stickiness of prices in goods markets, in order to model the phenomenon of exchange rate overshooting. However, the purpose of the Dornbusch–MF overshooting model was not to consider the dynamics of the external accounts, but of the exchange rate to explain observed exchange rate volatility. In this way, it provides an alternative to the monetary approach to exchange rate determination. Another feature of the Dornbusch exchange rate model is its demarcation between short-run and long-run effects of monetary expansion. This distinguishes the model from the earlier MF literature which was only concerned with short run adjustment issues.

Specification of External Accounts

Returning to the specification of the external accounts in the MF model, a further deficiency on this score is its failure to recognise the often quantitatively significant income and transfers sub-account of the current account which arises because capital inflows require servicing, particularly through interest obligations often payable immediately. In turn, growth in such payments widens the gap between national output and income according to national accounting principles, yet this crucial distinction is not normally drawn in comparative static applications of the basic MF model.

Nor does the MF model, in which the external accounts are expressed in domestic currency terms, recognize that changes in competitiveness arising from nominal exchange rate movements cause valuation effects for the current account of the sort discussed in Chapter 2. Relatedly, there are no J curve effects. This is because there are no export or import adjustment lags and the export and import demand elasticities are presumed to fulfil the Marshall–Lerner condition, such that depreciations quickly raise net exports whereas appreciations lower them. However, as Krugman (1989) argues, increased uncertainty about the sustainability of capital account driven depreciations is likely to frustrate any rise in net exports under a floating exchange rate regime. In particular, the link between depreciations and trade flows is likely to be weak or indeed non-existent because producers of exports and consumers of imports may quite rationally expect the exchange rate to rebound quickly and fully in the absence of any true or accepted model of short run exchange rate determination. This is of course as much a criticism of the relevance of the original elasticities approach as it is of the incorporation of the Marshall–Lerner condition in the MF model. It is also a criticism of the naive capital flow model of exchange rate determination in the MF model.

Even if we put aside the exchange rate uncertainty argument, but acknowledge valuation effects and J curves, a widened *CAD* must, according to accounting convention, be matched by capital inflow sufficient to match the increased *CAD*. In other words, if the widened *CAD* arises in the first instance because of a depreciation induced by capital outflow, there would then have to be an immediate reversal of capital outflow to capital inflow.

Neglect of Real Capital Accumulation

A more fundamental difficulty with the MF paradigm however is that it ignores the effect of foreign investment flows on the domestic capital stock, in much the same way as closed economy Keynesian models neglect the impact of domestic investment flows on the capital stock. In the closed economy case, allowing investment to matter for aggregate demand in the short run, but not matter for aggregate supply, has been justified on the grounds that while the purchase of capital goods immediately increases aggregate demand, it takes longer, because of installation lags, for the aggregate supply-side effects to become evident. Furthermore, it is argued that supply-side effects may be ignored because annual investment spending is a more significant portion of expenditure than of the existing capital stock.

However, these reasons for neglecting the supply side effects of investment can be challenged on the grounds that it seems quite unrealistic to assume that newly purchased, fully assembled capital equipment is rarely put to immediate use. Moreover, the suggestion that investment spending is not that significant relative to the value of the existing capital stock ignores the possibility that the most recently accumulated real capital is likely to have a higher marginal productivity than the pre-existing capital stock. Aggregate output or supply could also fall in the absence of replacement capital which is recorded in gross investment flows.

3.7 CONCLUSION

Although the MF model highlights the macroeconomic significance of the movement of international financial capital, it fails to embed these international financial flows adequately into real macroeconomic relationships relating domestic and foreign investment, domestic capital accumulation, rates of return on real capital and national income. Nor does it make saving and investment decisions central to external account determination.

National accounting however dictates that net capital inflow over any period can only occur if there has been a corresponding change in the nation's saving-investment imbalance, and relative wealth levels, the principal determinants of which should be explained in any general equilibrium model with reference to common real factors. Hence the emphasis in MF genus models on capital flows as purely financial phenomena, not directly tied to real phenomena, or intertemporal forces seems incomplete.

Financial capital flows as recorded in the capital account are not independent of the process of real international capital transfer, yet the MF model fails to capture this. On the other hand, output and expenditure decisions can indeed be independent of each other, as stressed by the absorption approaches, yet the MF model implies the opposite. In defence of the MF model, it may of course be argued that it was never designed to explain external account determination, but instead provides a starting point for analysing short run responses in income and exchange rates.

It is the purpose of the next chapter to survey and extend alternative approaches based on the accounting notion of the external imbalance as a nation's saving-investment imbalance. Such a perspective addresses many of the basic deficiencies of the MF and earlier approaches outlined above but which still pervade much of the recent literature on the external accounts.

4 Capital-theoretic Approaches to the External Accounts

4.1 INTRODUCTION

In broad terms, the traditional approaches to the external accounts outlined in the previous chapter, particularly the elasticities, absorption, and MF approaches stress expenditure and competitiveness as the chief determinants of the current account and restrict attention to the short-run implications of changing net exports of goods and services. Though the capital account plays a role in the MF approach, financial capital flows are not related to the real capital stock and hence the production side of the economy in any direct way. Indeed, a common factor uniting the earlier approaches is the general neglect of capital theory and the notion that there may be macroeconomic welfare gains from international trade in saving.

In contrast, this chapter brings capital theory to the forefront of the analysis of the open economy and external account determination. It reconciles a completely different set of international macroeconomic approaches to the theory of cross border capital movements by combining aspects of production, trade and finance theory. By focusing on the linkages between saving, domestic investment and foreign investment, it thus provides a sounder basis for understanding international capital mobility and external account determination in light of the aggregate accounting foundations of Chapter 2. It also allows us to highlight some important theoretical results which are central to later chapters. A primary aim is to demonstrate the macroeconomic gains from foreign investment by comparing the extreme cases of full capital mobility and capital immobility. This contrasts with the comparison between perfect capital mobility and capital immobility in the MF model.

The chapter proceeds as follows. First, the macroeconomic welfare gains from foreign investment and the relationship between real capital, national output, residents' standard of living and the external accounts are interpreted in the context of traditional foreign investment theory which abstracts from monetary factors. Following that, financial markets are introduced explicitly to further explain the process of international capital transfer. Then the intertemporal, or Fisherian, model is outlined, an approach which allows aggregate demand or absorption to change independently of aggregate supply or output. After this, some extensions to the intertemporal approach, including offer curve analysis, are presented. Finally, the intertemporal approach is reconciled with the accounting flow of funds, using a more general loanable funds framework to link saving, investment and the external accounts.

What distinguishes this chapter from the previous one is that the various approaches outlined in what follows share many crucial assumptions and hypotheses about the causes and significance of external account imbalance, whereas the approaches of the previous chapter are often at odds with each other. As with the earlier approaches to external account determination, however, there are a number of limitations to capital-theoretic approaches and these are discussed together before concluding the chapter.

4.2   THE TRADITIONAL FOREIGN INVESTMENT APPROACH

In parallel with the development of the MF and dependent economy models, a distinctly different, yet less widely adopted approach to the open economy emerged in the early 1960s, proposed by MacDougall (1960) and Kemp (1964, 1966).[1] Whereas the MF approach essentially stressed the aggregate demand side, this alternative approach stressed the supply side to explain the real macroeconomic effects of foreign investment from abroad on a host economy. It was based on Neoclassical assumptions, including perfect competition in goods and factor markets, full employment, and no external economies in production. As well, it often assumed constant returns to scale.[2] Interestingly, however, it was never intended to explain how the external accounts as such were actually determined; indeed originally there was no explicit mention of current account or capital account imbalances.

4.2.1   The Basic Model

Following Niehans (1984), consider an economy whose physical capital stock is small relative to the rest of the world's. In isolation, the economy's total gross output (Y) or aggregate supply of goods and services is determined by a macroeconomic production function, $Y = f(K,L)$, where K is the gross value of the capital stock and L is labour effort. Only real capital is free to move internationally, which permits abstraction from the economics of labour migration. It is also assumed the domestic labour force does not grow during the period of analysis.

Under competitive conditions in a closed economy whose initial capital stock is entirely owned by domestic residents, where the labour and goods markets clear instantly and where all output supplied by firms is demanded, the return to capital will equal its marginal product. Note that $f_k = \dfrac{\partial Y}{\partial K} > 0$ and $f_{kk} < 0$ by assumption. Initial output equilibrium is OD in Figure 4.1 where the slope of the production function reveals the marginal return on capital.[3] Aggregate gross income earned by capital is $f_k K$, as shown by distance AD.

Now if the foreign rate of return on capital (r^*) is lower than f_k, foreign investment (K^*) will eventually lead to an increase in the domestic capital stock to K_T, where $K_T = K + K^*$. Hence gross national

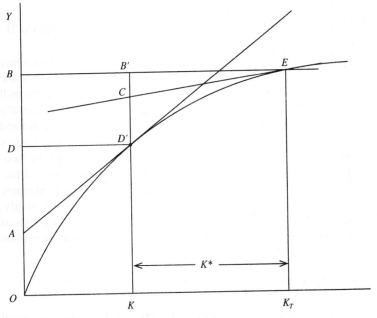

Figure 4.1   The gains from foreign investment (a)

output can be higher with foreign investment compared with autarky. $B'C$ is paid to non-residents, so gross national income rises by CD'.

The basic model outlined above may now be extended by relaxing the assumption about an exogenous world interest rate. Consider for instance, the case where, through foreign investment, one economic region is large enough to exert some influence on the productivity of capital, output and income in the other. Assume the two regions simultaneously move from autarky and permit foreign investment. They have similar production functions, as depicted in Figure 4.2, and the combined capital stock is shown by the length of the horizontal axis. Before free trade in real capital was permitted, economy A used its initial capital stock $O^A K^A$ to produce output equivalent to distance $O^A D$. Economy B used its relatively larger capital stock $O^B K^B$ to produce output equal to $O^B E$.

With full physical capital mobility, there would be a tendency for equalisation of the real rate of return on capital across both regions.

• W

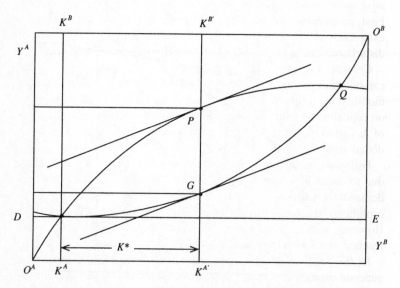

Figure 4.2   The gains from foreign investment (b)

Capital would move internationally until the marginal productivities of capital in the two regions equalise, having fallen in A and risen in B. In final equilibrium, additional capital accumulation in region A (K^*) through imports is matched by decumulation in region B through exports. Combined output rises by GP, or equivalently by $O^B W$. Had the autarky equilibrium for each region initially been at Q, the balances in the external accounts would have been reversed after allowing free trade in capital, with region B becoming the capital importer instead of A.

Though the neoclassical approach to foreign investment neglects the monetary implications of different exchange rate regimes as well as the balance of payments as such, it usefully illustrates the welfare gains from real capital transfers. In short, it reveals the benefits of full capital mobility over zero capital mobility where capital mobility is understood in a quite different sense to the MF approach.

4.2.2 Comparative Statics

To further educe the linkages between foreign investment, external balances, national output and national income, consider two comparative static exercises under the full real capital mobility assumption. First, an increase in domestic investment opportunities and second, an exogenous increase in the supply of foreign capital. Both forms of disturbance can at any time influence any nation's external accounts.

Consider Figure 4.3. In the figure, total wealth equals the combined capital stock throughout and, in initial equilibrium with full capital mobility, the return on capital is r. Since competition ensures the return on capital is the value of its marginal product, it follows that the value of A's gross output is the hatched area whereas gross output in B is the dotted area.

Following an increase in investment opportunities in A, for instance due to mineral resource discoveries in the home country, domestic demand for capital (I^A) would shift out. If foreign investment was prohibited, the return on country A's capital stock would rise to r'. However, with fully mobile real capital, it only rises to r'' which, when reached, is a Pareto optimum.

In the fully mobile case, greater investment opportunities in A generate capital imports of FG in the transition to the new equilibrium and equivalent capital exports for B. A continues importing real capital

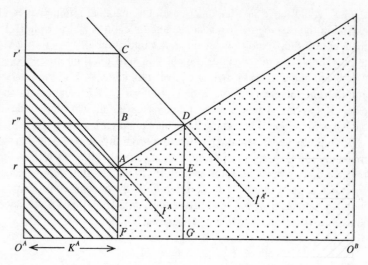

Figure 4.3   An increase in domestic investment opportunities

willingly exported by B, up to the point where the return on capital in both regions is again equalised.

What of the income effects? Interestingly, the free trade in real capital allows A and B's national income to be higher than otherwise, even though A's national output actually expands while B's contracts. The value of real income transfers eventually recorded as a debit item on A's current account is *FBDG*, the same amount accredited on B's current account. With full capital mobility, A's output is *FCDG* higher and national income *BCD* higher than if capital mobility was zero, while B's national output is *FADG* lower with national income *ABD* higher. Again, foreign capital helps A produce more domestic output since it augments the capital stock on the aggregate supply side of the economy.

The creation of higher income out of a fixed level of wealth necessarily dictates a rise in capital imports matched by rising capital exports abroad. In sum, with changing domestic investment opportunities and fixed wealth in terms of capital goods, the greater is real capital mobility, the higher the income gains may be for both regions.

Consider now the effects on trade in capital of an exogenous increase in B's wealth which enlarges total regional wealth by $O^B O^{B'}$, as shown

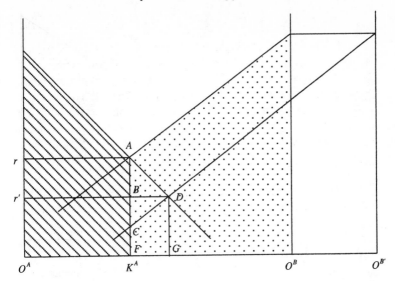

Figure 4.4   An increase in the supply of foreign capital

in Figure 4.4. Using similar reasoning, it again becomes clear that both A and B share the income gains when free trade in capital is permitted. The extra wealth enables additional output in A (area *ADGF*) and in B. A gains through the trade by area *ABD* while B gains by more than otherwise (area *BCD*). Combined income is *ADC* higher. Such an external disturbance generates a capital trade deficit for A and an equivalent capital trade surplus for B.

Two remaining disturbances could be analysed in this simple comparative static framework; first, a relative rise in A's wealth and second a relative rise in B's demand for capital. From an initial position of balanced trade, either disturbance would generate a trade surplus for A, matched by a capital trade deficit for B under the assumption of full real capital mobility.

4.2.3   Foreign Investment and Income Growth: Dynamic Analysis

Again, assume a small economy characterised by perfect competition, constant technology, constant returns to scale and full employment. Following Amano (1965), output (Y) is determined by an aggregate Cobb–Douglas production function of the form

$$Y(t) = K(t)^\alpha L(t)^{1-\alpha} \tag{4.1}$$

where K is the capital stock employed domestically, L is the amount of labour and α is the elasticity of output with respect to capital inputs. Under the above assumptions, α is also capital's share of total output. Therefore the domestic rate of return on capital is $\alpha Y(t)/K(t)$.

Further assuming that domestic saving is a constant fraction, γ, of national income and that labour effort is growing at a constant rate, n, then without capital mobility the output–capital ratio along the equilibrium growth path is $\dfrac{n}{\gamma}$, so that the rate of profit equals $\dfrac{\alpha n}{\gamma}$.

Assume now that the economy moves from zero capital mobility to full capital mobility at period 0. If the foreign rate of return on capital is r^*, then the economy will immediately import capital if $r^* < \dfrac{\alpha n}{\gamma}$.

If $K_T(t)$ is the total domestic capital stock, K^* of which is foreign-owned, then

$$K_T(t) = K(t) + K^*(t). \tag{4.2}$$

Following a move to full capital mobility, the domestic return on capital equates with the foreign return on capital. Therefore, it can be shown that

$$Y(t) = \frac{r^*}{\alpha} K_T(t). \tag{4.3}$$

Since $L(t) = L(0)E^{nt}$, it is possible to derive from (4.1) and (4.3)

$$K_T(t) = K(0)E^{nt}; \quad K_T(0) \equiv (0)\left(\frac{\alpha}{r^*}\right)^{\frac{1}{1-\alpha}}. \tag{4.4}$$

As we know, national income (Y_n) is the difference between output and interest paid abroad

$$Y_n(t) = Y(t) - r^*K^*(t). \tag{4.5}$$

Lastly, we can express the saving–investment imbalance as

$$\gamma Y(t) + \frac{dK^*(t)}{dt} = \frac{dK_T(t)}{dt}. \tag{4.6}$$

Using (4.3) and (4.4) and substituting (4.5) into (4.6) yields

$$\frac{dK^*(t)}{dt} - r^*\gamma K^*(t) = \frac{dK_T(t)}{dt} - \gamma Y(t)$$

$$= \left(\frac{\dfrac{dK_T(t)}{dt}}{K_T(t)} - \gamma \frac{Y(t)}{K_T(t)} \right) K_T(0) E^{nt}$$

$$= \left(n - \frac{r^*\gamma}{\alpha} \right) K_T(0) E^{nt}. \tag{4.7}$$

Equation (4.7) is a non-homogeneous first order linear differential equation in $K^*(t)$ whose general solution is given by

$$K^*(t) = C_1 E^{nt} + C_2 E^{r^*\gamma t} \tag{4.8}$$

where

$$C_1 \equiv \frac{n - \dfrac{r^*\gamma}{\alpha}}{n - r^*\gamma} K_T(0) \qquad \text{and}$$

$$C_2 \equiv K_T(0) - C_1.$$

$C_1 > 0$ since $n > r^*\gamma/\alpha$ and $\alpha < 1$ by assumption. C_2 can be re-expressed as

$$C_2 = \frac{(1-\alpha)r^*\gamma}{\alpha(n - r^*\gamma)} K_T(0) - \frac{n - \dfrac{r^*\gamma}{\alpha}}{n - r^*\gamma} K(0)$$

$$= \frac{\gamma}{n - r^*\gamma} \left(\frac{1-\alpha}{\alpha} r^* K^*(0) - \left(\frac{n}{\gamma} - \frac{r^*}{\alpha} \right) K(0) \right). \tag{4.9}$$

If $Y_0(0)$ is the value of national income which would have been produced at period 0 without foreign investment, then

$$Y_0(0) = \frac{1}{\alpha} \left(\frac{\alpha n}{\gamma} \right) K(0) < Y(0) = \frac{r^*}{\alpha} (K(0) + K^*(0)) - r^* K^*(0)$$

or

$$\frac{1-\alpha}{\alpha} r^* K^*(0) - \left(\frac{n}{\gamma} - \frac{r^*}{\alpha}\right) K(0) > 0.$$

(4.10)

From (4.9) and (4.10), it follows that $C_2 > 0$.

The time path of national income may be derived from (4.3), (4.4), (4.5) and (4.8)

$$Y_n(t) = \frac{(1-\alpha)nr^*}{\alpha(n-r^*\gamma)} K_T(0) E^{nt} - C_2 r^* E^{r^*\gamma t}.$$

(4.11)

Therefore, we can express the rate of growth of national income, $g(t)$, as

$$g(t) \equiv \frac{dY_n(t)}{dt} \Big/ Y_n(t) = n + \frac{C_2 r^* E^{r^*\gamma t}}{Y_n(t)} (n - r^*\gamma).$$

(4.12)

As $C_2 > 0$, it follows from (4.12) that $g(t) > n$ for $0 \leq t < \infty$. However, $g(t)$ declines through time as $C_2 r^* E^{r^*\gamma t}/Y_n(t)$ diminishes. Finally, $g(t) \rightarrow n$ as $t \rightarrow \infty$.

Therefore, we can conclude that with a move from autarky to full capital mobility, the rate of growth of national income is transitionally higher than the equilibrium growth rate (n) in the very long run.

4.2.4   Interest Rates and Financial Claims to Capital

So far, no mention has been made of financial claims to capital, since the analysis of the gains from foreign investment has been strictly in real terms. By introducing financial claims to capital however, it is possible to shed further light on the dynamics of capital transfer across national borders with unrestricted foreign investment. As in the traditional foreign investment approach without financial claims, it is assumed that in the home country, capital is not produced specifically for deployment abroad.

As proposed by Niehans (1984), all capital income may be in the form of dividends paid on equities (q), each one of which represents a claim to a unit of a country's capital stock. The yield is therefore $r = f_k/q$. In initial autarky equilibrium, the market value of the capital stock (q) at home and abroad should be the same as its replacement cost ($\overline{q}$) in accordance with Tobin's q theory of investment.[4]

If the replacement cost of capital goods is the same in the host economy as abroad, but initially $\dfrac{f_k}{q=\bar{q}} > \dfrac{f_{k^*}}{q^*=\bar{q}}$, then the domestic yield on capital must be higher than the foreign yield. Foreign investors are now able to purchase domestic securities issued in the home country. Consistent with the theory of international trade in goods, free trade in financial capital, in the absence of uncertainty and transactions costs, will ultimately establish a common price, in this case the yield on capital, which will clear the unified markets.

With unrestricted foreign investment, the process of trade in financial claims immediately drives up the market value of the capital stock in the home country above replacement cost to equalise interest rates, thus eventually inducing the transfer of real capital from abroad; that is, $r = r^* \Rightarrow q > \bar{q}$. In the final equilibrium, after unrestricted foreign investment has been allowed, $q = \bar{q}$, but this may take some time given that real capital must be imported and installed. As additional units of capital are put into production, the domestic return on capital continues to fall since $f_{kk} < 0$. No further real capital is imported when the market

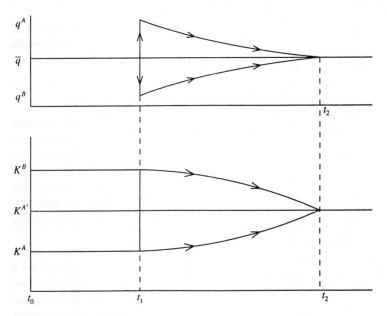

Figure 4.5   Time paths for q and K

value of capital again equals its original replacement value, at which time the marginal product of capital is the same transnationally.

In the two-region case of Figure 4.2, full capital mobility with financial claims means an initial increase in q above replacement cost in country A, whose capital is relatively more productive, and a fall in q in country B. The corresponding time paths of adjustment of the market values of claims to capital and the capital stock itself are shown in Figure 4.5. Given the initial accumulation and distribution of capital, the opening up at time t_1, of free trade in financial and real capital leads to a jump increase as q rises in A and q falls in B. As long as $q^A/\bar{q}$ is greater than unity in A and $q^B/\bar{q}$ is less than unity in B, capital will be exported by B and imported by A until the market value of capital again reflects its replacement value at time t_2.

4.3   THE INTERTEMPORAL APPROACH

In the above we examined the international macroeconomic consequences of liberalising foreign investment and demonstrated the welfare gains from full capital mobility. In the traditional approach however, the capital stock is simply determined by the given wealth level and as a single sector approach, it fails to allow for intersectoral borrowing and lending, consistent with the accounting flow of funds framework of Chapter 2. Nor does it allow for forward looking behaviour.

An alternative, although essentially compatible capital-theoretic approach to international capital movements and the external accounts extends the analysis of foreign investment using the precepts of intertemporal trade developed by Fisher (1930).[5]

4.3.1   The Basic Model

In a two sector economy, comprised of households and firms, it can be assumed that aggregate output and expenditure are determined separately as in the earlier absorption approach of Chapter 3. Firms invest and combine labour, land, existing capital and given technology to produce maximum output over two periods of time (the present and the whole of the future), whereas households have preferences for present consumption (C_1) versus future consumption (C_2) and supply labour inelastically. Once again, the analysis abstracts from capital stock depreciation.

Central to the intertemporal approach is the notion of an investment opportunities function (*f*) which transforms forgone present consumption (saving) into future output (Y_2) through additional capital accumulation (investment I_1). The transformation curve is defined as $F(Y_1, Y_2) = 0$ and the intertemporal production function is of the form $Y_2 = Y_1(K, L) + f(I_1)$. To fix ideas about the intertemporal approach, let us present some basic optimising conditions, initially in the closed economy context. These conditions form the basis for subsequent diagrammatic analysis for the open economy.

The economy's problem is to maximise its consumption or living standards (*l*) intertemporally, given present output and the available investment opportunities. The economy's utility function is therefore $l(C_1, C_2)$. The present values of the future stream of output (Y_2) and consumption (C_2) are $\dfrac{Y_2}{1+r}$ and $\dfrac{C_2}{1+r}$ where *r* is the prevailing domestic interest rate. Output produced by firms over both periods, $F(Y_1, Y_2)$, is maximised and the solvency condition for households is that income received over both periods is sufficient to fund the intertemporal consumption pattern; that is, $Y_1 + \dfrac{Y_2}{1+r} = C_1 + \dfrac{C_2}{1+r}$. All of the output produced by firms is consumed by households over the two periods, and the Lagrangean $L(C, Y, \lambda)$ is:

$$L(C_1,C_2,Y_1,Y_2,\lambda_1,\lambda_2) = l(C_1,C_2) + \lambda_1\left(Y_1 + \left[\frac{Y_2}{1+r}\right] - C_1 - \left[\frac{C_2}{1+r}\right]\right) + \lambda_2 F(Y_1,Y_2).$$

Therefore the first order conditions state

$$D_1 L = D_1 l - \lambda_1 = 0 \tag{4.13}$$

$$D_2 L = D_2 l - \left(\frac{1}{1+r}\right)\lambda_1 = 0 \tag{4.14}$$

$$D_3 L = \lambda_1 + \lambda_2 D_1 F = 0 \tag{4.15}$$

$$D_4 L = \left(\frac{1}{1+r}\right)\lambda_1 + \lambda_2 D_2 F = 0 \tag{4.16}$$

$$D_5 L = Y_1 + \left[\frac{Y_2}{1+r}\right] - C_1 - \left[\frac{C_2}{1+r}\right] = 0 \tag{4.17}$$

$$D_6 L = F(Y_1, Y_2) = 0. \tag{4.18}$$

From (4.13) and (4.14) it follows that for households

$$MRS = \frac{D_1 l}{D_2 l} = 1 + r$$

and for firms from (4.15) and (4.16)

$$MRT = \frac{D_1 F}{D_2 F} = 1 + r.$$

Hence, $MRS = MRT$, or the marginal rate of substitution of present for future consumption equals the marginal rate of transformation of present into future income.

4.3.2 Diagrammatic Analysis with Full Capital Mobility

With these results as a basis, we can again depict the welfare gains from foreign investment under conditions of full international capital mobility using a Fisherian framework. In Figure 4.6, if present period saving is zero, then in a certain world with unchanged production technology, output 'endowed' in the future would be the same as in the present (as conveyed by the 45° line). With positive saving, however, the productive investment which abstinence allows yields higher future output and hence income, as determined by the investment opportunities frontier capturing domestic firms' ability to transform current income into future income. As in the previous neoclassical approach, the marginal productivity of capital declines when more domestic capital is combined with the available supply of other resource inputs.

If capital is immobile internationally, the equilibrium return on capital for the economy would be determined by the intersection of investment opportunities and households' saving propensities. Hence, in equilibrium both the economy-wide return on capital and households' rate of time preference would equal the real interest rate. The slope of the investment opportunities curve and the consumption indifference curve would be 1+r at the point of tangency. Therefore, if nations' capital markets are isolated, the range of international interest rates would reflect the diversity of national saving propensities and investment opportunities.

However, with a move from zero capital mobility to full capital mobility, the correspondence between aggregate domestic saving and investment would be broken. The Fisher separation theorem, which suggests that financial markets enable consumption and investment decisions to be made independently,[6] would therefore hold in an international macroeconomic setting. Moreover, in the absence of un-certainty, and abstracting from the complication of changing exchange rate expectations, domestic and foreign claims to real capital would become perfect substitutes. Through arbitrage, a small country's inter-est rate should equate with the prevailing world interest rate such that capital becomes perfectly mobile in the sense used earlier in the MF model. There are other measures of capital mobility, however, and the complete set of these conditions will be fully defined in the following chapter.

Figure 4.6 also illustrates the macroeconomic benefits of full capital mobility over zero mobility, yielding similar results to the traditional approach. If the autarky interest rate is initially higher than the world interest rate (r^*), full capital mobility necessarily creates a saving–investment imbalance, thus generating a *KAS* for the financially open economy. With reference to the figure, domestic capital formation rises by distance *KS* since investment continues up to the point where the rate of return on capital equals the foreign interest rate.

The exact response of present consumption to interest rate changes is, however, a matter of some theoretical controversy. A fall in the interest rate makes current consumption less expensive relative to future consumption, discouraging saving – the substitution effect. On the other hand, the reduced income from interest receipts encourages households to save more – the income effect. Pre-Keynesian econom-ists assumed the dominance of the substitution effect making current saving a rising function of the interest rate, but in theory this ambiguity cannot be resolved as Bailey (1957) demonstrated.

Assuming the dominance of the substitution effect, saving falls by distance *AS*, with point *E'* to the north-east of the initial consumption point. If, however, the income effect dominated, the new consumption point would lie north-west. In the case where the substitution and

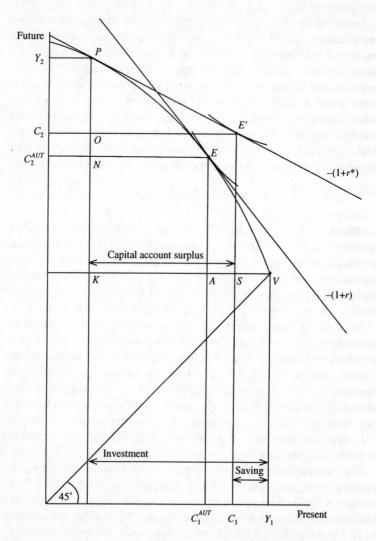

Figure 4.6   Intertemporal gains from foreign investment (a)

income effects offset, the new equilibrium would lie directly above the old. Foreign investment in the small country is matched by a collective *CAS* run by the rest of the world and is equivalent to distance *KA* in the first period, the difference between domestic saving (*AV*) and domestic investment (*KV*).

Under the lower world interest rate regime, the equilibrium optimising condition is $MRS = MRT = 1 + r^*$. Income and consumption both today and tomorrow can be higher than under zero capital mobility, again affirming that foreign investment under full capital mobility improves the economy's standard of living. Provided initial expectations about the income producing potential of capital are fulfilled, future income will always be adequate to repay the external financial liabilities run up to finance the higher domestic capital accumulation. This is because, geometrically, distance *OP* in Figure 4.6 will exceed distance *OE'* as long as the interest rate is positive, since the slope of the budget line must then exceed unity; that is, $\dfrac{OP}{OE'} = 1 + r^* > 1$.

The process of real capital transfer associated with the foreign investment recorded on the capital account is matched on the current account by either imported investment goods or imported consumption goods which release resources for domestic capital production. Since introducing intermediate goods would considerably complicate the analysis, we have implicitly assumed throughout that all goods are final goods.

As with the traditional approach, we can move from the small economy to the two region case, whereby interest rates become endogenously determined. Figure 4.7 shows the effects of integrating the capital markets of two previously autarkic regions with different investment opportunities and saving propensities. After allowing unrestricted foreign investment, arbitrage again ensures a single interest rate. Country A's initial interest rate falls and country B's rises.

Living standards rise in both countries and the equilibrium condition is that $MRS^A = MRS^B = MRT^A = MRT^B = 1 + r'$.

The external account triangles suggest that a move to full capital mobility from zero mobility creates capital inflow or a *KAS* of *FG* in country A matched by capital outflow or a *CAS* of *IJ* in B. To repay its international obligations in the future, economy A transfers *EF* income to B. Unambiguously, foreign investment under full capital mobility raises living standards in both regions because the trade in saving

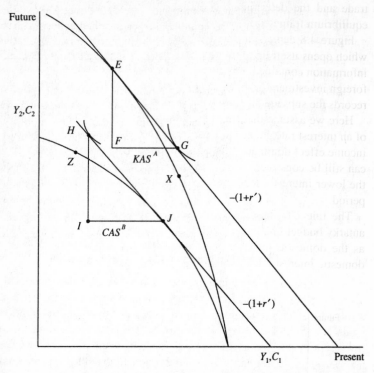

Figure 4.7   Intertemporal gains from foreign investment (b)

allows households to reach higher levels of welfare compared with those possible in isolation; that is, for country A, $G > X$ and for country B, $H > Z$.

4.3.3   Offer Curve Analysis

The intertemporal approach to foreign investment provides a basis for introducing offer curves, usually only employed in the pure theory of international merchandise trade, to model the external accounts. Casting the intertemporal approach in terms of offer curves serves to highlight that, contrary to the approaches to the external accounts outlined in Chapter 3, international trade in saving essentially determines the external balances with consequent real effects. It also demonstrates that there are important similarities between the pure theory of international trade and the determination of the external accounts in a general equilibrium framework.

Figure 4.8 depicts an intertemporal offer curve for a small country which opens itself up to international trade in saving. It is based on the information contained in Figure 4.6. The horizontal axis records inward foreign investment or the present period *KAS*, whereas the vertical axis records the subsequent *KAD* which will be generated.

Here we assume that the substitution effect on present consumption of an interest rate change at least offsets any income effect. Even if the income effect dominated the substitution effect, however, offer curves can still be constructed, provided the extra investment stemming from the lower interest rate exceeds any additional consumption in the first period.

The line *UU′* has the same slope in absolute value terms as the autarky budget line in Figure 4.6. Foreign investment continues to rise as the domestic interest rate approaches the world rate. When the domestic interest rate equals the world rate as shown by line *WW′*, the

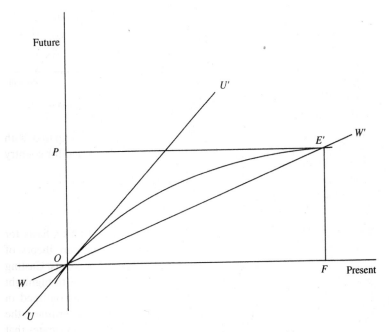

Figure 4.8 Intertemporal offer curve (a)

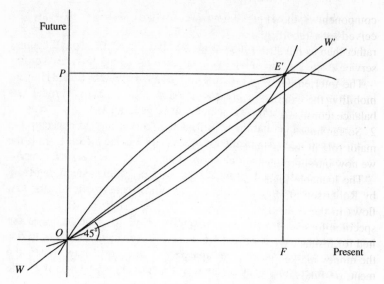

Figure 4.9   Intertemporal offer curve (b)

small country imports *OF* of foreign saving in period one, which it later repays with interest as *OP*. The triangle *E'OP* is the same as the intertemporal trade triangle *E'OP* in Figure 4.6.

In the two-region case, the general equilibrium outcome is shown in Figure 4.9. The intersecting ray must lie above the negative 45° line, whose slope equals unity, if the interest rate is to be positive.

In parallel with orthodox international trade theory, the offer curves demonstrate that when foreign investment is allowed and capital markets are fully integrated, a common price, the return on capital, must prevail, and this price clears the unified markets. Foreign investment confers welfare gains if economies' real interest rates would be different without trade. Economies would not engage in intertemporal trade, however, irrespective of the extent of capital mobility, if domestic interest rates were identical in autarky.

4.4   THE LOANABLE FUNDS APPROACH

The traditional and intertemporal approaches to foreign investment outlined above suggest that a country's external accounts, as a component of the larger framework of social accounts, are best perceived as a record of international capital flows between countries, rather than as the difference between exports and imports of goods and services.

The intertemporal approach explicitly recognizes that with capital mobility, the external accounts are a nation's saving–investment imbalance, consistent with the accounting flow of funds matrix of Chapter 2. So far however, liquid funds as such have not been afforded any major role in the capital centred approaches. To remedy this omission, we now introduce the loanable funds model.

The loanable funds theory of interest rate determination advocated by Robertson (1940), amongst others, explicitly recognises financial flows in the context of saving and investment behaviour. Originally specified for a closed economy, the loanable funds approach as exposited for instance by Tsiang (1989) suggests that on the demand side of the money market, there are d^1 funds required to finance firms' investment, d^2 funds required to finance firms' replacement capital (that is, depreciation reserves), d^3 funds to be added to inactive balances held as liquid reserves (that is, hoarding), and d^4 funds required to finance households' consumption in excess of disposable income (that is, dissaving).

On the supply side, there are s^1 funds due to the excess of households' disposable income over planned consumption expenditure, s^2 depreciation reserves taken out of firms' gross sales of the preceding period, s^3 funds used from previously held inactive money balances (that is, dishoarding) and s^4 funds representing the net creation of additional money by banks. In an open economy, again consistent with our earlier flow of funds matrix (Table 2.1), we can add s^5 funds provided by the rest of the world.

The equilibrium condition for the total demand and supply of loanable funds is then

$$d^1 + d^2 + d^3 + d^4 = s^1 + s^2 + s^3 + s^4 + s^5$$

which can be rearranged as

$$\underbrace{\frac{I}{d^1 + d^2}} - \underbrace{\frac{S}{(s^1 + s^2 - d^4 + s^4)}} + \overbrace{\underbrace{d^3 - s^3}^{Net\ Hoarding}} = \overset{KAS}{s^5}$$

If we write it this way, we can see how the flow record of external imbalance relates to the demand and supply of loanable funds.

Domestic and foreign money may be directly supplied by households and by non-residents to domestic firms for investment purposes via the purchase of equities and debt instruments from firms. Or excess funds may be supplied indirectly via financial intermediaries.

The loanable funds perspective also recognises hoarding activity, or changes in demand for inactive cash balances, the basis for which may be explained by the precautionary and speculative motives, first outlined by Keynes (1936). In this way, the approach provides a link to the monetary underpinnings of the MF model. Though we abstract from hoarding behaviour in what follows, on the assumption that hoarding is relatively insignificant in relation to gross saving and investment flows, it is of interest to note that an increase in hoarding (dishoarding) should increase (decrease) the *KAS* if the demand for investible funds exceeds the domestic supply.

Since domestic saving equals households' lending and since domestic firms' investment equals borrowing at home and from abroad, the earlier intertemporal framework can now be entirely translated to the present period analysis of the loanable funds approach.

In Figure 4.10, firms' demand for funds becomes a decreasing function of the interest rate, whereas the supply of funds lent by households becomes an increasing function of the interest rate. We continue to abstract from the effects of exchange rate expectations and assume all variables are expressed in real terms. The investment possibilities frontier of the intertemporal framework suggests that domestic firms will borrow funds if the interest rate is less than the return on additional real capital accumulation. The slope of the saving schedule is positive if the substitution effect dominates the income effect.

Schedule *AA'* in the left panel shows economy A's excess demand for saving (its *KAS* or *NFI*) for given interest rates with full capital mobility. If the economy is small and the foreign interest rate is r^*, the *KAS* is *OW* because the supply of foreign saving is perfectly elastic at any rate below r^A, the autarky interest rate. A fall in the world interest rate would, *ceteris paribus*, therefore raise the small country's *KAS*.

In the two region case, schedule *BB'* is introduced to show B's excess supply of saving (*CAS*) for interest rates above r^B, B's autarky interest rate. This framework may now be used to predict the impact on the external accounts of various exogenous shocks. If, for instance, a decrease in time preference abroad raises foreign saving, the *BB'* schedule would shift down to *BB''*, lowering the equilibrium interest

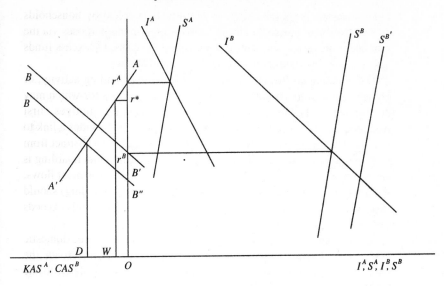

Figure 4.10 Loanable funds and foreign investment

rate for both countries. A's *KAS* rises to *OD* to match B's *KAD*. Similarly, it can be shown quite easily that a fall in the demand for investible funds in B has the same effect. Hence, with unrestricted foreign investment, A's *KAB* can also be determined entirely by changes in investment and saving behaviour in B. The shared external imbalance can also change as the result of shifts in the *AA′* schedule. *AA′* shifts down, narrowing the *KAS*, when either A's investment falls or its saving rises. Hence, the extent of foreign investment can depend on either internal or external macroeconomic disturbances.

4.5 LIMITATIONS

Like the traditional approaches of the previous chapter, capital theoretic models of the external accounts also have limitations which, for balance, should be canvassed. For instance, the single sector traditional approach is entirely static, and hence neglects the importance of expectations. While this deficiency is addressed in the two sector Fisherian approach, agents are there, somewhat unrealistically, assumed to have perfect foresight with no role for uncertainty in the model. Yet some of the key variables in the intertemporal analysis are by nature inherently uncertain – for instance, the expected productivity of capital and hence future income streams.

The location of firms' actual investment possibilities frontier is perhaps better understood as lying within a range, the size of which is determined by the degree of uncertainty. Moreover, the position of the frontier changes whenever there are supply shocks or changes in technology.[7] Households are also uncertain about the future income on which they base their consumption plans. If future income happens to be less than expected, consumption may therefore prove unsustainable. Alternatively, there will be disequilibrium if income is higher than expected.

The intertemporal approach as outlined above also neglects public sector activity and hence does not explicitly allow for an interpretation of the effects of fiscal policy on the external accounts. However, fiscal policy can be analysed easily enough within the more general loanable funds framework. For instance, we can consider the effects of fiscal changes on either the S^A or I^A schedules of Figure 4.10 where these schedules now represent total domestic private and public saving and total domestic private and public investment.

If there is a fall in public saving following fiscal expansion, the S^A schedule should shift to the left, widening the external imbalance, assuming full capital mobility. Similarly, a rise in public investment expenditure could shift the I^A schedule to the right, increasing the KAS. We also see in the following chapter, that capital is not fully mobile in reality, as just assumed in arguing this line of causality between the two deficits. Note that the line of causality is however an alternative to the causal chain implied by the MF model.

Many other underlying assumptions of the capital-theoretic approaches can also be questioned. For instance, prices may not adjust rapidly to clear the goods markets in the background, firms and labour unions may exercise monopoly power and there may be price signalling distortions in both goods and financial markets due to externalities. Furthermore, if international capital movements increase in response to distortionary capital income tax measures, then macroeconomic welfare may in fact be lower, not higher as a consequence of any induced capital movements.

The above models also abstract from the business cycle under the assumptions of market clearing and price flexibility ensuring unemployment is at the 'natural rate' at all times. As output is essentially supply side determined through a macroeconomic production function, the approaches are sharply at odds with the Keynesian inspired MF approach covered in the previous chapter, which stresses factors affecting aggregate demand, including the fiscal and monetary policy instruments at the disposal of the authorities. While many of the above assumptions may be technically difficult to relax in capital-theoretic approaches, such relaxation is unlikely to change the broad conclusions about the welfare gains from capital mobility.

By not affording a role to the central bank, another serious omission of the capital centred models of the external accounts and the open economy is that they fail to explicitly account for the effects of monetary policy and the generation of inflation, although as we saw in the previous chapter, by and large neither do the other more traditional open economy approaches. The approaches interpreted above also somewhat unrealistically put exchange rate considerations aside and hence totally abstract from the impact of competitiveness on exports and imports.

4.6 CONCLUSION

In this chapter, international capital movements were examined using general equilibrium models for a small economy facing a fixed world interest rate or, in two country versions, capital mobility was considered in cases where the common interest rate was endogenous. In addition to highlighting the macroeconomic gains achievable through foreign investment, this chapter demonstrated how capital account balances were determined.

However, the foregoing analysis of the welfare effects of foreign investment presumed financial and real capital was perfectly mobile in the sense that cross-border real rates of return on capital equalised in the absence of uncertainty. In practice however, foreigner's ignorance of investment opportunities abroad, the phenomena of country risk, exchange rate risk, tax treatment of earnings on foreign investment and widespread exchange controls restricting capital movements may combine to ensure different national rates of return on capital.

5 Capital Mobility and the External Accounts

5.1 INTRODUCTION

After the collapse of the Bretton Woods system of exchange rate management, a range of deregulatory actions affecting domestic and international financial transactions were implemented, including the abolition of capital controls and interest rate ceilings, as well as the entry of foreign financial institutions into domestic markets. These policy initiatives, combined with technological progress in telecommunications, and widespread financial innovation, greatly reduced transactions costs and broke down barriers separating economies' financial markets.[1]

Historically, the process of capital market integration began gathering pace from the mid-1970s with the relaxation of capital controls in the United States and Canada. By the end of the 1970s, the United Kingdom had abolished its exchange controls and, throughout the 1980s, Japan gradually relaxed restrictions on foreign outward investment by institutional investors. Financial market liberalisation in most OECD nations was virtually complete by the late 1980s. With the removal of what were previously quite stringent regulations over domestic and international financial transactions, institutional barriers impeding the movement of financial capital within the OECD area have now largely disappeared.

Both domestic and international financial transactions had been tightly controlled for much of the postwar era. For instance, at the domestic level there were often quantitative limits on bank lending and deposit and lending rates were sometimes directly controlled by central banks. A range of capital controls also impeded international financial flows, including prohibitions on capital outflows and embargoes on short-term inflows. With the abolition of such restrictions throughout the 1980s, external borrowing and lending began to rise sharply.

Financial deregulation proceeded apace in industrial economies essentially because there was widespread acceptance that microeconomic efficiency gains could be realised by removing domestic interest rate distortions and by fostering increased competition between financial intermediaries. Accompanying the domestic deregulatory changes were strengthened prudential supervisory arrangements. Capital backing of banks became the basis of prudential regulation from the late 1980s in line with guidelines issued by the Bank for International Settlements. These set out the appropriate ratio of capital reserves banks were obliged to hold against risk weighted assets and were intended to strengthen the capitalisation of banks and hence the security of the financial system.

It may be argued that the deregulation of domestic financial transactions could have produced a once-only increase in consumption, because consumer credit became more readily available. However, in practice, private saving rates in many OECD economies remained fairly stable over the period, even though financial liberalisation may have altered the nature of the consumption function itself, making aggregate consumption less responsive to income fluctuations because of the easing of households' liquidity constraints.

Moreover, it is possible that the quality of domestically financed investment could have risen because domestic deregulation improved the allocation of domestic saving, allowing it to finance more profitable investment opportunities. It is also true that some deregulatory measures had direct implications for both domestic and international financial transactions. For example, the licensing of an increased number of foreign banks in domestic markets increased competitive pressures generally at the same time as it facilitated domestic firms' access to new channels of foreign saving.

The volume of both capital inflows and outflows increased in the 1980s in the new deregulated environment and the single most significant deregulatory measure which contributed to this was the abolition of many postwar controls over the international movement of financial flows. There was also greatly increased fundraising through the Eurodollar markets which was not, of itself, a product of deregulatory measures adopted by industrial nations at home but a consequence of institutional developments outside the sphere of traditional financial markets.

In short, the abolition of official restrictions governing cross-border transactions transformed the financial markets of OECD economies from being heavily regulated and segmented into ones that were lightly regulated and internationally integrated. Access to international financial capital and services increased greatly throughout the 1980s. This boosted borrowing and lending opportunities and implied that capital mobility was enhanced relative to earlier decades.

5.2   MODELLING INTERNATIONAL CAPITAL MARKET INTEGRATION

In Chapter 4 we used the intertemporal approach to the external accounts to demonstrate the welfare benefits of full capital mobility against capital immobility. Elements of that approach can now be applied to model the stock adjustment effects of international financial liberalisation which more closely integrated national capital markets.

Whereas much of the foregoing discussion of the external accounts canvassed influences on flow magnitudes determining the external accounts in the 1980s, this section shifts attention to aggregate stocks. In particular, it shows how the international financial liberalisation of the 1980s may affect a nation's external indebtedness position, as well as the value of its capital stock and wealth.

To illustrate the effect of international financial liberalisation on investment, foreign debt, the capital stock and wealth, consider Figure 5.1 below. The analysis is initially restricted to firms' behaviour. As in Chapter 4, we invoke an investment opportunities frontier which

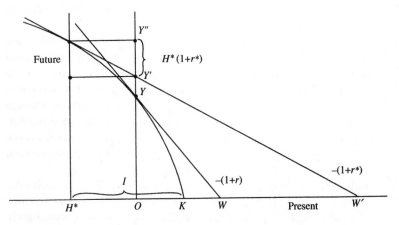

Figure 5.1   International financial liberalisation and external debt

captures firms' ability to transform current investment into a future stream of income. Here, however, we focus for the first time on the stock adjustment aspects of increased capital market integration and assume all variables are expressed in real terms.

With prohibitive exchange controls in place, domestic investment would only proceed up to the point where the return on capital, net of depreciation, was equal to the domestic interest rate, r. In the figure, investment would be K and the present value of the future income stream would be W. In a certain world with a competitive capital market and no transactions costs, the present value of firms' investment is also the market value of the firms' common shares, which in this simple model equals the value of the economy's assets. Optimal investment decisions by firms maximise the net present value of investment and also maximise the value of national assets.

After dispensing with exchange controls and other institutional impediments to foreign investment, it is possible for firms to borrow at a lower rate of interest (r^*) prevailing in international capital markets.

With reference to the above figure, domestic firms borrow H^* abroad after deregulation which then becomes a stock adjustment increase in foreign debt. By investing $K + H^* = I$, firms generate future income of Y'' the present value of which is $Y''/(1 + r^*)$ or $H^* + W$. However, since H^* plus $r^* H^*$ in interest must eventually be paid to foreign lenders, the future income accrual to residents shrinks to Y'. The present value of the future income stream to domestic residents is

$$\frac{Y'' - H^*(1 + r^*)}{(1 + r^*)} \text{ or } W'.$$

Hence this approach implies that, under conditions where external borrowing is freely permitted and cheaper funds are available from somewhere abroad, an increase in external indebtedness funding additional real investment should lead to a rise in the value of national wealth, provided the increase in the present value of the capital stock as reflected in equity prices exceeds the increase in external indebtedness.

Put another way, the increase in external liabilities is more than offset by an increase in the market value of assets, such that national wealth rises, where national wealth is defined as the difference between national assets and external liabilities. Note from the figure that this must be so since the increase in the future income stream made possible by the external borrowing $Y'' - Y$ exceeds future repayments, $H^*(1 + r^*)$.

Also consider the dynamics of the increase in real investment in terms of the q theory exposited in Chapter 4. Since $r = f_k/q$ initially, with a lower foreign interest rate, q will immediately increase, raising the market price of capital above its replacement cost. This induces the additional real investment, which eventually lowers the marginal product of capital.

Though the emphasis so far has been on the use of external borrowing to finance additional domestic investment, the intertemporal model also shows that it is possible to increase the value of national assets and hence national wealth if the foreign loans are used to finance investment abroad. In such a case, national wealth increases if the net present value of the additional investment abroad exceeds the value of the foreign borrowing used to finance it.

In summary, this simple variation of the Fisherian approach of Chapter 4 suggests that, other things equal, international financial market liberalisation may lead to an equalisation of domestic and foreign interest rates, immediate stock adjustment, as reflected in a sharp increase in external debt, but also a rise in national wealth.

To simplify exposition, the above discussion ignored the effects of increased capital market integration on national saving. As discussed in Chapter 4, the impact of changes in the interest rates on saving is somewhat ambiguous in a theoretical sense, since there may be off-setting income and substitution effects. If the substitution and income effects of a fall in the cost of capital exactly offset each other, present saving becomes inelastic with respect to the interest rate.

Using this assumption, which is standard for instance in textbook discussion of closed and open economy Keynesian models, where the interest rate is not an argument in the consumption function, we can explicitly incorporate saving into Figure 5.1 by imagining consumption indifference curves tangential to points Y and Y'. The wealth levels OW and OW' then represent the net present value of additional future consumption stemming from additional investment.

The above model also implicitly assumes 'fundamental valuation efficiency' which according to Tobin (1984) prevails when the prices of financial claims to capital accurately reflect all future payments to which those claims give title. Many would argue, however, that 'fundamental valuation efficiency' does not always prevail, as evidenced by the phenomenon of speculative bubbles followed by sharp collapses in asset markets such as occurs in stock markets from time to time.[2] This then raises perennial and complex questions about the nature of expectations formation and financial market efficiency, and indeed the very worth of financial market activity.[3] Many of these issues remain, and perhaps will always remain, unresolved and a full discussion lies beyond the scope of this chapter. Suffice to say that we presume over longer periods, such as a decade, that the valuation of the private capital stock is at least roughly efficient, in an 'on average' sense and that financial markets are not persistently prone to waves of irrational behaviour.

Nonetheless, it is still possible to capture the effects of well founded revisions to expectations about future income streams in the above model. If, for instance, expectations were suddenly revised upwards on the basis of new information about investment prospects, the investment opportunities frontier would bow upward from the origin. Though not drawn in the figure above, it is relatively straightforward to demonstrate that, under the assumptions of the approach, an upward revision of investment prospects would further increase foreign debt, investment and national net worth, provided foreign lenders concurred with the upward revisions. If they did not, a risk premium would then be added to the foreign interest rate on offer, limiting the investment, capital stock and external debt increase.

The effects of increased capital market integration on the external accounts can also be shown in terms of the simple flow of funds framework used earlier. For instance, with reference to Figure 5.2, if capital controls were initially prohibitive, the domestic interest rate would be domestically determined at real interest rate r, corresponding to the intersection of the interest inelastic saving schedule, and the downward sloping investment schedule.

Following deregulation which permits foreign borrowing at a lower real interest rate, the domestic real interest rate would fall to r^*, the foreign real interest rate. Simultaneously, there would be a rise in investment financed by foreigners, and hence a rise of AC in the capital account surplus. If capital was initially only partially mobile, on account of quantitative capital controls which limited foreign borrowing to the extent of distance AB, then the interest differential would be $r' - r^*$, which should disappear after the abolition of exchange controls. If the nation was initially a net debtor, saving would be defined as domestic saving, that is, net of interest payments paid on previously accumulated external debt. It also follows that the wider is

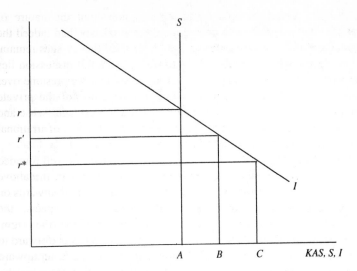

Figure 5.2   Capital market integration and the external accounts

the initial interest differential, the lower is the correspondence between domestic saving and investment at a given level of income.

5.3   FURTHER DEFINING CAPITAL MOBILITY

A unifying theme of Chapters 3 and 4 was the macroeconomic significance of capital mobility. In Chapter 3, for example, we saw that the polar assumptions of perfect versus imperfect mobility yielded markedly different results about the effectiveness of policy instruments in the MF model. In the MF model, perfect capital mobility relates bond yields across borders, although, as mentioned in Chapter 3, this approach fails to allow for exchange rate expectations which are implicitly assumed static. This implies that the international equalisation of interest rates is essentially determined in the first instance by the interaction of stock domestic money demands and supplies. With fixed price levels, nominal and real equalisation of interest rates is the same.

In contrast, Chapter 4, which outlined capital theoretic approaches to the external accounts, showed that full capital mobility, understood in both a real and a financial sense, unambiguously raised a nation's standard of living when compared to zero capital mobility. Similarly, capital mobility was characterised by the international equalisation of interest rates, but in the models of Chapter 4, the real interest rate, as a measure of the return on the capital stock, was determined by real forces including the eventual international transfer of physical capital. Both Chapters 3 and 4 highlighted the significance of capital mobility by considering polar extremes. But how do we actually measure international capital mobility and to what extent did international financial liberalisation enhance it?

When considering the extent of international capital market integration, an important distinction is that between international asset substitutability and capital mobility.[4] If economic agents are indifferent between holding financial securities at home or abroad for given yield differentials and exchange rate expectations, the assets are perfectly substitutable. The extent of capital mobility governs whether economic agents may achieve desired portfolio holdings and in practice is limited by factors such as ignorance of foreign investment opportunities and the phenomena of country, political and exchange rate risk.

The degree of capital mobility may be tested against a range of conditions.[5] The most comprehensive set of conditions for gauging capital mobility would include (1) closed interest parity, (2) covered interest parity, (3) uncovered interest parity, (4) real interest parity and (5) the extent of correlation between changes in domestic saving and investment (as proposed by Feldstein and Horioka, 1980).

Closed interest parity obtains if financial capital flows equalise interest rates across borders when debt instruments are denominated in a common currency. Covered interest parity holds when the difference between the forward and spot exchange rates entirely reflects interest differentials on debt instruments denominated in different currencies. If covered interest parity does not hold, this suggests there are unexploited profit opportunities from interest arbitrage. Assuming arbitrage, the above equality will only fail to hold exactly if there is uninsurable risk, large transactions costs or exchange controls.

Uncovered interest parity (UIP) holds when capital flows equalise expected rates of return on bonds denominated in different currencies, after allowing for exchange rate expectations. It may be expressed as $i - i^* = s_e$ where s_e is anticipated currency depreciation, i is the domestic nominal interest rate and i^* the foreign nominal interest rate.

For UIP to hold empirically ex post, we must assume that agents are risk-neutral and that observed nominal interest rates incorporate a premium for (rationally) expected future exchange rate movements. Alternative forms of UIP assuming, say, adaptive expectations could conceivably hold ex ante, though most specifications jointly propose risk neutrality and rational expectations in testing the relationship.

Real interest parity is simply the equalisation of real interest rates, $r = r^*$. For real interest parity to hold, however, both UIP and purchasing power parity (PPP) must hold. A simple proof of this is as follows. Since real ex ante interest rates at home and abroad are $r = i - \pi^e$ and $r^* = i^* - \pi^{e^*}$ (where π^e and π^{e^*} are the expected inflation rates at home and abroad), it follows that the real interest differential is $r - r^* = i - i^* - \pi^e + \pi^{e^*}$. Since the UIP condition is $i - i^* = s_e$ and ex ante PPP is simply $\pi^e - \pi^{e^*} = s_e$, both UIP and PPP must hold exactly and at all times to equalise real interest rates internationally.

Another test of capital mobility ascribed to Feldstein and Horioka (1980) adopts a quite different perspective to the above conditions, which test capital mobility by measuring returns on debt instruments. The Feldstein–Horioka (FH) interpretation of capital mobility focuses on aggregate investment–saving imbalances and suggests that if international capital markets are highly integrated then there is likely to be little correlation between increases in the level of saving in one particular country and that country's level of investment.

Another way of putting this is that, in an open economy, saving and investment behaviour should be independent of each other in the spirit of the Fisher separation theorem as explained in Chapter 4. If saving is free to move internationally, it will be used to finance additional investment around the globe with little used to finance extra investment at home. The FH proposition has been perceived as an alternative measure of capital mobility and has spawned an extensive empirical literature.

In their original paper, Feldstein and Horioka empirically tested an equation for OECD economies of the form $I/Y = a + bS/Y + \varepsilon$, where a and b are coefficients, ε is a stochastic error term and the other nominal variables are as earlier defined. In short, they suggested b should be zero if capital was perfectly mobile. However, Feldstein and Horioka's evidence of a high correlation between domestic saving and investment levels for OECD countries implied a low level of international capital mobility with results for the period 1960–74 showing that domestic

saving passed into domestic investment (the 'savings retention coefficient') almost one to one. Subsequent empirical studies tended to
confirm this.[6]

The FH approach to measuring capital mobility was subsequently
criticised by several authors. For instance, some claimed that, to minimise divergences between domestic saving and investment, governments tended automatically to react to current account imbalances
through fiscal responses by changing public saving and investment to
offset external account imbalances.[7] This 'policy-reaction' argument is
the 'twin deficits' hypothesis in another guise.

More recent studies[8] have addressed many of the theoretical and
empirical criticisms levelled against the original FH methodology and
found that, although the savings retention coefficient had fallen for
OECD countries throughout the 1980s, it was still higher than would be
expected in a world of high capital mobility. High saving–investment
correlations cannot, however, be interpreted in isolation as evidence of
imperfect capital mobility since the FH definition of capital mobility
only holds if real interest parity holds and the real interest rate is
determined exogenously to the country in question.

To demonstrate why the interest parity conditions and the small
country assumption are necessary and sufficient for the FH condition,
consider Figure 5.3 below. Assume a small economy is initially in

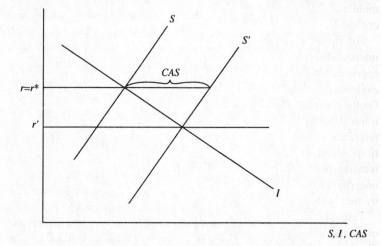

Figure 5.3   Interest parity and the FH condition

equilibrium, saving equals investment and all of the parity conditions outlined above are fulfilled, so that $r = r^*$.

According to the FH proposition, perfect capital mobility would obtain if, following an increase in domestic saving, foreign outward investment increased by distance *CAS*, the size of the external surplus. However, for this to occur all other conditions for capital mobility must be fulfilled, since the domestic interest rate must still equal the foreign rate.

Alternatively, if capital is completely immobile according to the FH proposition, the additional saving generates increased investment at home and, instead of capital outflow, the domestic interest rate falls below the world rate. In light of the analysis of foreign investment in Chapter 4, macroeconomic welfare is maximised if a *CAS* is generated, but is suboptimal if immobility prevails and the interest differential widens.

5.4 EMPIRICAL EVIDENCE ON CAPITAL MOBILITY

The empirical evidence on capital mobility in the wake of the widespread liberalisation of financial markets suggests that capital mobility increased in OECD countries during the 1980s and was indeed highly mobile if judged against some but not all of the above capital mobility criteria.[9]

For instance, on the basis of the closed interest parity condition, interest differentials on Eurocurrency borrowings had largely disappeared for the major OECD countries by the mid 1980s. There is also evidence of covered interest parity holding for many OECD currencies.[10] On the contrary, the international evidence does not support uncovered interest parity.[11] This failure of UIP can perhaps be explained with reference to time varying risk premia and irrationally formed expectations about exchange rate movements, the determination of which remains poorly understood. Yet it seems plausible that exchange rate uncertainty has increased during the floating era, characterised as it is by such wide nominal exchange rate fluctuations.

Tests of real interest parity also reveal that, internationally, the degree of co-movement of real interest rates has not increased markedly since the onset of financial liberalisation, nor has the real interest differential narrowed by as much as could be expected.[12] However, there has been some narrowing of real interest differentials consistent with increased capital mobility. Nonetheless, given the failure of UIP to hold and the overwhelming evidence against PPP, particularly over shorter periods, it should not be surprising that real interest parity also fails to hold, for, as derived above, UIP and PPP are preconditions for real interest parity.

Finally, several empirical studies have confirmed that, on the basis of the FH measure, capital mobility increased in the 1980s.[13] Further evidence of a weakening of the correspondence between nations' saving and investment behaviour is simply provided by the worldwide increase in external imbalances.

In summary, though it appears that capital mobility still lies somewhere between the polar extremes used as a pedagogical device in earlier chapters, the empirical evidence suggests that, on balance, capital mobility increased substantially in the wake of international financial liberalisation. Capital mobility remains less than perfect because increased exchange rate volatility under floating rates has tended to reduce financial asset substitutability; other reasons would have to include the inherent riskiness of foreign investment, the threat of the reimposition of official capital controls and remaining institutional practices which ensure that part of domestic saving is directed largely towards financing strictly domestic activity, as for example with private household saving lodged with specialised financial institutions such as building societies.

Furthermore, some direct foreign investment may occur more for the purpose of overcoming goods and services trade restrictions than of strictly obtaining a higher rate of return on capital.[14] There is also evidence that fund managers of large institutions have actively sought to diversify asset holdings internationally in order to minimise risk due to uncertain returns.[15] Hence, in practice, consistent with standard portfolio theory, capital flows may be driven to a large extent by the expected variance of returns on capital and not just the return itself.

Though it was argued in Chapter 4 that the greater is capital mobility, the greater the macroeconomic welfare gains, there is a contrary view which suggests capital mobility has now become 'excessive'. Tobin (1978), for instance, echoing Keynes' (1936, ch. 12) views on the inherent irrationality of financial markets, raises concerns about destabilising exchange rate movements which cause sustained deviations of real exchange rates from fundamentals, with adverse implications for domestic inflation, output and employment.

As a remedy, Tobin proposed that international capital mobility be limited by throwing some 'sand on the wheels' of the international financial system; specifically, by imposing a worldwide financial transactions tax of 1 per cent on the value of any spot conversion of one currency into another. However, it would obviously be difficult to apply such a tax consistently worldwide. More importantly, the proposal ignores the macroeconomic welfare losses that could result if foreign capital, irrespective of its maturity, is prevented from flowing to areas where it earns its highest risk-adjusted rate of return.

5.5   SAVING, INVESTMENT AND THE EXTERNAL ACCOUNTS

So far in this chapter, capital movements in relation to saving and investment behaviour have largely been considered without reference to changing national income levels. Instead, the focus has been on the international equalisation of returns on capital, as measured by interest rates, with allowance for exchange rate expectations.

Attention now turns to evaluating possible economic determinants of domestic saving and investment themselves with reference to a simple absorption-inspired theoretical framework which is consistent with the models of the previous chapter. This explicitly allows us to consider shifts in saving and investment and their implications for the external accounts in the context of growing national output. Influences canvassed in what follows include shifting demographics, both domestically and internationally, increased profitability, fiscal activity and monetary policy.

5.5.1   Determinants of Saving and Investment

Chapter 4 stressed that the external account imbalance is best understood as the difference between domestic saving and investment. This suggests that it may be illuminating to examine determinants of saving and investment behaviour separately in order to explain external account outcomes. In other words, what domestic and external influences may affect domestic saving and investment, and hence the external imbalance?

To assist understanding in this regard, consider Figure 5.4 below, frequently referred to in the subsequent discussion of this section.

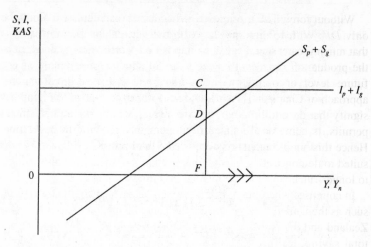

Figure 5.4   Saving, investment and the external accounts

Domestic saving is depicted in this diagram as an increasing function of output and hence national disposable income, whereas investment opportunities are presumed autonomous. All variables are expressed in real terms.

Contrary to the closed economy case, where the level of national saving fully constrains investment spending, this framework again shows that, in a financially open economy, domestic investment, both private and public, may be independent of domestic saving. The difference between ex ante investment and saving determines the current and capital account balances at any level of output.

Unlike the loanable funds approach of the last chapter, it explicitly allows for changing national income levels and, contrary to the MF model of Chapter 3, it is consistent with the absorption approach, since changes in domestic expenditure at given output levels immediately affect the external imbalance. Although saving is shown as an increasing function of income, the S schedule need not necessarily depict a simple Keynesian saving function, as usually assumed in the MF approach, for example. If, for instance, the horizontal axis was relabelled 'permanent income', the S schedule would still be upward-sloping, but would pass through the origin.

Without foreign investment, domestic capital accumulation would be only *DF*. With foreign investment, however, capital accumulation is that much greater and, as real capital, net of depreciation, is an input to the production process, this extra capital should further increase the future level of output, a result consistent with the intertemporal approach of Chapter 4. The arrows on the horizontal axis of Figure 5.4 signify that the additional productive capital, which foreign investment permits, is being accumulated in an economy growing through time. Hence this simple model abstracts from the business cycle and is best suited to demonstrating the external account consequences of medium- to longer-run changes in saving and investment.

In countries where there had been significant financial liberalisation, such as the United States, Canada, the United Kingdom, Australia, New Zealand and the Nordic countries, the household saving component of total saving declined significantly in the 1980s. Indeed, in Finland, Norway and Sweden, net household saving ratios became negative.[16] However, these falls in household saving tended to be offset by rises in business saving, leaving gross private saving, the aggregate of most interest from an international macroeconomic perspective, largely unchanged.[17] Furthermore, the empirical evidence suggests that neither movements in interest rates nor the strong rise in private sector wealth in OECD countries over the 1980s had any effect on short-run saving behaviour.[18]

In economic policy circles, it is often suggested that external deficits of countries like the United States, Canada and Australia are a manifestation of domestic saving being 'too low'. Hence, by implication, policy measures should aim at shifting the saving schedule of Figure 5.4 upward to narrow the perceived problem of the external imbalance being 'too high'. But is such thinking misplaced in light of the fundamental determinants of domestic saving behaviour?

For example, demographic factors may be an important influence on saving patterns through time, both across countries and within countries. If the age composition of the population changes, so too will saving, insofar as consumption behaviour differs between different age groups. Consider the case of a nation which experiences a fall in the proportion of the population of working age and an associated rise in the proportion of retirees. If retirees have a higher consumption to income ratio, then, consistent with the 'life-cycle' hypothesis (Ando and

Modigliani, 1963), this could result in some fall in private saving, causing a downward shift of the *S* schedule of Figure 5.4.

Another demographic factor which could conceivably affect both domestic saving and investment behaviour is immigration, to the extent that it increases population growth, alters consumption patterns and creates a demand for additional capital to accommodate and employ the extra population.

Significant differences in age profiles, combined with the nature of the social security system and the way it provides for retirement, are likely to account for at least part of the difference between saving rates across countries. For instance, many OECD nations have generous publicly funded pension schemes, yet Japan, for example, does not. Hence the high rate of Japanese saving over the 1980s may have been partly determined by the forward-looking consumption behaviour of a significant component of its population. Japan has been a major source of capital inflow for many nations; to the extent that demographic factors raised Japan's saving, it was an exogenous determinant of other nations' external imbalances. That is, increased capital outflow from Japan meant more domestic investment opportunities were exploited by domestic firms in other nations either borrowing part of this 'excess' foreign saving or by Japanese firms investing directly. With reference to Figure 5.4, total foreign investment and the investment schedule in host countries rose simultaneously.

Microeconomic distortions, due for instance to the nature of a nation's taxation system, may also make domestic saving less than optimal. The same may be said of tax systems abroad which make saving more than optimal.

A fundamental determinant of private domestic investment is corporate profitability, a direct indicator of which is the ratio of gross operating surplus to the capital stock, that is $\dfrac{GOS}{K}$, an average measure. A higher profit share, to the extent that it raises the rate of return on capital may give rise to an adjustment period characterised by buoyant investment and output growth. As an ex post average measure of the rate of return on capital $\dfrac{GOS}{K}$ is, however, an imperfect proxy for the relative ex ante marginal rate concept used in the open economy capital theory of the previous chapter. Desirably, other macroeconomic rates of return on capital, such as relative earnings–price ratios for equities across country borders, should also be considered, but data limitations often prevent this.

Sustained increases in profitability usually improve the ratio of the market valuation of companies to the replacement cost of capital. According to the *q* theory of investment outlined in Chapter 4, rises in *q* should of themselves stimulate additional real investment and therefore induce real capital transfer from abroad.

In sum, then, unexploited investment opportunities may initially be reflected in rising *q* values for companies listed on domestic stock exchanges. If so, in terms of our Figure 5.1, this suggests an economy's investment schedule would shift upward and, as long as the additional investment is willingly financed by foreigners, it manifests as higher foreign investment.

Foreign saving may be borrowed by either domestic or foreign-controlled firms to finance additional investment in host countries; this is essentially the portfolio versus direct foreign investment distinction defined in Chapter 2. Though foreign direct investment entails loss of control of corporate assets, it usually generates important benefits, including technology transfer, international management expertise and product innovation.[19]

With direct investment, the investment and funding decisions are often made simultaneously by multinational corporations. Therefore increased imports of capital goods recorded on the trade account may be matched at the same time by financial capital inflow to directly finance their purchase, though of course this will not necessarily occur. If it does, the extra supply of foreign exchange can therefore be used directly to purchase additional imported capital goods; hence, under these circumstances, there is unlikely to be any effect on the exchange rate attributable to a change in the net flow demand for foreign currency.

5.5.1 Fiscal Policy and Ricardian Equivalence

As suggested by the MF model of Chapter 3 and the loanable funds model of Chapter 4, the 'twin deficits' hypothesis, irrespective of the exact nature of the theoretical linkages, ultimately depends on unchanged private saving behaviour in the face of increased fiscal deficits and rising public debt.

The transmission mechanisms of these models are, however, subject to the ambiguities raised by the Ricardian Equivalence (RE) theorem.

This theorem is based on David Ricardo's suggestion that tax and bond financing of government expenditure may equivalently affect private consumption spending even though Ricardo himself dismissed the idea.[20] Essentially, in generalised form the RE proposition is based on households' perceptions of government bonds held in their investment portfolios. An increase in bond holdings may not imply an increase in financial wealth, since bonds also represent the future obligation of the government which the private sector will ultimately have to meet through higher taxes. Hence an increase in public debt outstanding as a result of higher budget deficits arising from either increased government spending or reduced taxes should therefore lead to higher private saving in preparation for the future tax burden. If private agents care as much about their descendants' economic welfare as about their own, it does not even matter if the future taxes will not be levied in their own lifetime.

This proposition in its strict form suggests that the scope for active fiscal policy is non-existent. Contrary to the traditional Keynesian approach, which asserts that individuals treat tax cuts like any other form of income, budgetary measures intended to stimulate private spending would be immediately offset by reduced spending as economic agents recognise that fiscal expansion, budget deficits and higher public debt levels imply future tax increases. In terms of the *IS–LM–BP* diagram, the RE proposition suggests that government attempts to shift the *IS* curve prove futile, thus eliminating any link between the public and external accounts.

In terms of the saving–investment models, if RE held in a strict sense, there would likewise be no effect on the external imbalance because, with either increased public consumption or investment, there would be an offsetting fall in private consumption at given levels of output. With increased public consumption widening the public account deficit, RE implies no net change in the position of the S^A schedule from Figure 4.10, whereas with increased public investment it implies that any rightward shift in the I^A schedule is matched by a rightward shift of the S^A schedule, leaving the external imbalance unchanged at the prevailing interest rate. In practice, only if RE does not hold on a one-for-one basis would there be a link between domestic fiscal and external deficits.

Although the RE proposition in its strict form negates the 'twin-deficits' application of the MF model, it seems plausible that practical considerations forge a firm link between the deficits, to the extent that agents have incomplete information or less than rational expectations. Indeed, it may even be rational for some agents to expect future tax increases not to apply to them personally and hence not adjust their behaviour. Furthermore, there is the possibility of reverse causality between the public and external accounts contrary to the line of causality proposed by the 'twin-deficits' hypothesis. For example, in the event of a foreign-financed private investment boom, the *KAS* would rise but, other things equal, the budget deficit would tend to surplus as tax revenue increased because of rising incomes.

Moreover, changes in taxes or public spending may, through incentive effects, alter private sector saving and investment behaviour in other ways. Hence RE may be necessary but not sufficient for a one-to-one relationship between the consolidated public account and the external imbalance.

There is also empirical evidence that private and public saving are imperfect substitutes, contrary to the RE proposition, such that variations in the fiscal stance are likely to have affected external account outcomes by altering the pattern of public saving and investment.[21]

In terms of Figure 5.1, the failure of the RE proposition to hold implies that changes in public saving shift the total *S* schedule about: downwards, for example, during fiscal expansions and associated falls in public saving and upward during fiscal contractions and rises in public saving. To the extent that domestic fiscal policy affects a nation's total saving, it must also be acknowledged that fiscal policy abroad affects the availability of foreign capital. In this regard, it is noteworthy that there was strong fiscal consolidation in Japan and Germany throughout the 1980s, which should have augmented the total supply of capital available for domestic and foreign use in those countries. The reverse was true, however, for the United States in light of its relatively loose fiscal stance.

Fiscal restraint may lower public investment as well as public consumption, but if reduced public investment is more than offset by rising private investment, the total investment schedule of Figure 5.4 could still shift upwards in net terms by more than the increase in total saving, resulting in a wider external imbalance.

However, this outcome ignores conceptual issues about whether a large part of public expenditure is more appropriately classified as investment rather than consumption. For instance, to the extent that increased health and education spending, now defined in OECD national accounts as public consumption, improves the productivity of the human capital stock, it could be considered as contributing to increased public investment, rather than lower public saving. Though recent patterns of public saving and investment in OECD economies would look quite different if reclassified this way, *ceteris paribus*, the size of recorded foreign investment flows would nonetheless remain the same. Total saving might be less affected by the swings in recorded public saving shifting the total saving schedule of Figure 5.4, but instead there would have been greater offsetting variation in public investment shifting the total investment schedule in the opposite direction.

5.5.3 Monetary Policy

How changes in the stance of monetary policy affect the external accounts under floating exchange rates and highly mobile capital is a largely unresolved theoretical issue. As argued in the preceding chapters, existing models are somewhat ill equipped to deal with the consequences of monetary expansions and contractions for the external accounts in an integrated way.

The MF approach, for instance, is most often used to predict the external consequences of monetary policy changes and, as outlined in Chapter 3, this model under the perfect capital mobility assumption implies that the trade account tends to surplus (deficit) following a monetary expansion (contraction). The main channel of influence is through financial capital flows affecting the nominal exchange rate and hence net exports by virtue of the Marshall–Lerner condition. However, the MF transmission mechanism provides a less than satisfactory understanding of the process of external account determination, for the many other reasons already outlined in Chapter 3. If financial capital is less than fully mobile in the MF sense, questions then arise as to the impact of domestic interest rate changes on total expenditure and hence imports. Additionally, whenever the monetary stance tightens, there is the further complication of the net income paid abroad component of the *CAB* increasing, owing to rising interest payments on domestic currency debt owned by foreigners.

Whether monetary policy has in practice affected the nation's external accounts any differently in the financially deregulated era, compared with the earlier regulated one, can be clouded by disagreement over the actual stance of monetary policy at any given time. For instance, lower inflation rates combined with higher real short-term interest rates in the OECD could indicate that the 1980s was not a decade of easy money relative to the 1970s.

Short-term interest rates were also considerably more volatile and higher than long-term rates throughout the 1980s, with inverse yield curves providing further evidence of the overall tightness of monetary policy. On the other hand, it could be argued that monetary policy tended to be quite expansionary at times throughout the 1980s, as indicated by relatively high money base growth coinciding with stronger sustained output growth.

The short-term and long-term influence of domestic monetary policy on the external accounts raises important questions for further study about the nature of the linkages between the money supply, inflation, interest rates, exchange rates and the external accounts themselves.

5.6 CONCLUSION

Over recent years, financial liberalisation throughout the OECD region, along with continued innovation in the Eurocurrency markets, improved access to alternative saving and investment possibilities and the degree of international capital mobility therefore increased. However, the enhanced mobility of capital and global integration of financial markets was a facilitating, not motivating, factor behind the growth and persistence of external imbalances, the size of which was essentially determined by changes in national saving and investment behaviour.

6 Policy Issues and Conclusion

6.1 INTRODUCTION

As highlighted in Chapter 1, the global phenomenon of the widening of external account imbalances, particularly from the early 1980s, was usually interpreted in negative terms. For many nations with external deficits, such as Australia, Canada, Britain and the United States, imports were often popularly considered to have been too high relative to exports, gross national expenditure too high relative to gross national product, and domestic saving too low relative to investment. For surplus countries, such as Japan, exports, GDP and saving were deemed too high relative to imports, expenditure and investment. Such views reflect the different ways of presenting the external imbalance as set out in the international macroeconomic accounting framework of Chapter 2.

6.2 FALLACIES ABOUT SAVING AND INVESTMENT

For instance, the absorption equation which expresses the external imbalance as the excess of expenditure over output, provides a basis for the common assertion that nations experiencing current account deficits were 'living beyond their means'. This phrase implies that, as for an individual household, national spending can not be sustained beyond national income. Yet, as demonstrated in earlier chapters, the pure absorption equation has no explicit intertemporal dimension. Since it fails to distinguish between consumption and investment expenditure, it can therefore be misleading. Almost by definition, OECD nations with current account deficits were not consuming beyond their means in the 1980s, because over the same period they generated significant positive saving.

Figure 6.1 below shows relative saving and investment behaviour in the OECD area for the 1980s. The vertical distance between the point shown for any country and the diagonal line in the figure is

111

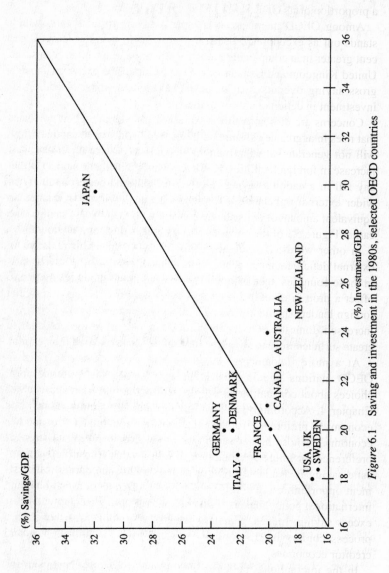

Figure 6.1 Saving and investment in the 1980s, selected OECD countries

approximately the value of the country's external account imbalance as a proportion of its GDP.

Among OECD members, it is Japan's saving to GDP ratio which stands out as exceptional, because it is so high, being at least 50 per cent greater than comparable ratios for Australia, the United States, the United Kingdom and Canada. A rising portion of the excess of Japan's gross saving over its own domestic investment financed additional investment in deficit countries in the 1980s.

Concerns are also sometimes expressed in external deficit countries that rises in aggregate consumption, financed by increased capital inflow will not generate sufficient national income to service any associated increase in foreign liabilities. However, what such claims neglect is that any fall in a nation's saving can only be reflected correspondingly in wider external imbalance if foreigners are also willing to finance an equivalent amount of domestic investment with their excess saving. The earlier Figure 5.1 of the previous chapter makes this point obvious.

In other words, if foreigners' propensity to finance investment in external deficit countries remains unchanged, yet domestic saving falls in those countries, then capital inflows would not automatically rise to offset a drop in domestic saving. What is not often understood is that foreign lenders should always be making judgements about whether the increased domestic activity their funds finance have the potential to create sufficient revenue to allow for eventual repayment of their capital.

At a more fundamental level, however, private saving rates in OECD nations should have revealed households' intertemporal choices about consumption, as proposed by the Fisherian approach of Chapter 4. Accordingly, a 'low' saving rate then simply reveals one economy's preference for current consumption relative to another economy's whose higher saving rate may simply reveal its stronger preference for future consumption. It follows that if insufficient domestic saving is available in some nations to finance domestic investment opportunities, then this should not be of concern to national and international policy makers if other countries bridge the gap with their excess saving. Indeed, a major theme of this book, was that such a process confers macroeconomic welfare gains on both debtor and creditor economies.

In the international policy debate about saving-investment imbalances, questions often arise about the nature of investment activities that foreign funds finance, specifically whether foreign capital is always directed toward expanding tradable or non-tradable activities. Notwith-standing some of the difficulties with classifying activities as between tradable and non-tradable, a number of points can be made against the proposition that the kind of investment financed matters in any case. First, some non-tradable activities (for example, business services) are probably best thought of as complementary to tradable activities, so that foreign investment in such areas may well ultimately improve the overall competitiveness of tradable industries. Second, foreign funds may directly finance the creation of new tangible assets which would not otherwise be created, as for example with real estate development, and the creation of such assets may simply be motivated by the prospect of a capital gain on the sale of the asset to other foreigners, with no undesirable economic consequences for the host nations.

Indeed, foreign investment in the form of purchases of existing property puts upward pressure on all property values. In this way, foreign investment in property can actually improve national wealth. Residents of nations who sell existing property assets to non-residents obtain capital gains which would not otherwise have occurred, though of course such capital gains are excluded from conventional measures of residents' national income. Third, in any event a part of any nation's foreign debt may actually be denominated in domestic currency which makes it unnecessary to eventually generate foreign exchange for the extra activity that part of foreign debt financed.

Fourth, as also argued by Pitchford (1990), any nation's external debt level should not, of itself, be considered an international macro-economic problem, unless sources of market failure can be identified which may have distorted external debt levels above and beyond those normally incurred in the process of financing private investment.

6.3 POLICY ISSUES

The absolute value of external debt levels in OECD nations sometimes creates anxiety because it is sometimes interpreted as a sign of inter-national insolvency. National balance sheets constructed in accordance with the framework mentioned in Chapter 2 would, as a rule, show otherwise, however. Moreover, comparisons of the external debt positions of OECD members with those of Latin American and East European economies also abound, despite the relatively small share of sovereign or official debt within the total external debt of many OECD nations and despite the absence of any explicit official underwriting of private sector debt, as often occurs in other debtor countries with less sophisticated capital markets. The external debt of OECD nations should also be distinguished clearly from that of Latin American countries because official international financial institutions such as the IMF and World Bank have not been involved directly.

Of course, it may then be argued that the monetary authorities provide implicit guarantees to large external debtors and would assume a significant share of external liabilities in the event of widespread servicing difficulties. However, it remains a matter of conjecture as to whether, and to what extent, such guarantees would be applied, even in extreme circumstances, such as a severe global recession.

A fundamental inconsistency in international macroeconomic policy in the 1980s arose because it was usually not recognised that continuing capital inflow and rising external imbalances were being jointly determined. Global financial deregulation facilitated greater international investment flows, yet the external imbalances which were a manifestation of these flows sometimes became targets of macroeconomic policy.

Why was this? If it was because the overall level of economic activity became too buoyant, and inflation was too high, then the problem was excess aggregate demand, not widened external imbalances.

If national monetary authorities in external deficit countries thought domestically based business enterprises became too careless about offshore borrowing the most direct policy response would have been the reimposition of exchange controls prohibiting such activity. But of course, the reduction of capital inflow would, other things equal, have immediately put downward pressure on the exchange rate and, more generally, have lessened central banks' capacity to influence competitiveness through the interest rate channel. In any case, such a re-regulatory policy would not have been advisable in view of the micro-efficiency arguments originally proposed to support widespread financial deregulation.

The salient feature of the rise in external indebtedness in many OECD countries was that much of it was incurred by private enterprises in host countries, irrespective of whether they were owned and controlled by residents or non-residents. Hence it should have been taken for granted that private firms committed to servicing their overseas borrowings also rationally assessed ex ante whether the income stream generated through the use of foreign capital would have been sufficient to meet repayments. To suppose otherwise was tantamount to questioning whether private firms generally acted to maximise profit. In this regard, to say rising external indebtedness was in some way a national problem meant enterprises which borrowed offshore were mostly mistaken.

At the microeconomic level, as long as firms operating in external deficit countries contracted loans with offshore lenders and paid lower interest (inclusive of exchange rate effects) than the return on additional productive investment, then transitional growth rates were higher. If they did not, losses were made, and at the macroeconomic level, investment fell reducing the external imbalance. In short, foreign investment flows, irrespective of their form (debt or equity participation), in net terms enabled external deficit countries to finance that much more investment which, for given domestic saving, enlarged the capital stock of those economies and allowed them to produce more output than otherwise.

Obviously there were instances where domestic firms 'over-borrowed' offshore or, what amounted to the same thing, cases where foreigners unwisely invested their funds in host countries. Moreover, there were grounds for doubting whether all public business enterprises which may have borrowed heavily abroad after deregulation used their foreign funds prudently. At a basic level, problems encountered for such firms arose because the future profitability of the enterprises was uncertain at the time loan contracts were struck. What was important however were not isolated, yet usually well-publicised, cases of individual private and public companies in financial difficulty but whether public and private firms with external liabilities, in the aggregate, were profitable in the sense that the real return on foreign capital exceeded its servicing cost.

To be less than sanguine about firms' ability to achieve such a result in truth revealed misgivings about the nature of capitalism itself. An essentially Keynesian view of the world therefore applies to the extent that the central authorities assume a highly activist role in stabilising the economy because goods, services and financial markets do not ensure macroeconomic stability.

Though it is normally assumed in host countries that the business sector's domestic financial liabilities are used productively, the monetary authorities often implicitly assume otherwise about their external liabilities. Yet domestic lenders lend against a firm's collateral and foreign lenders in principle act no differently. In extreme cases where resident firms found they were too overgeared to service external debt, liquidators were called in to wind them up. By and large, it was immaterial under such circumstances whether troubled firms' liabilities were to residents or to foreigners. Assets were sold and part of the external debt disappeared.

One possible side-effect of greater external borrowing, which should be acknowledged as a caveat to earlier arguments, is that larger foreign loan raising by more adventurous firms could raise the interest rate risk premium charged to all other borrowers. Corden (1991) for instance has stressed this 'contamination' effect in his thorough search for qualifications to the so-called 'new view' of the external accounts.

The most fundamental reason for the persistence of external account imbalances in the 1980s, however, was that aggregate savings and investment behaviour differed within and between nations. While this may suggest public policy initiatives in external deficit nations to encourage greater domestic saving, attempts to change saving behaviour permanently may well be frustrated, since consuming less out of disposable income would lower the short run living standards of households.

To the extent that households do not behave as predicted by the Ricardian Equivalence proposition and raise private saving to offset any budget deficit induced fall in domestic saving, it could be argued that an appropriate fiscal policy response to any rising external imbalance would be to achieve greater budget surpluses. However, as Corden (1991) again notes, the macroeconomic policy issue then becomes not whether external deficits per se are excessive, but whether the budget imbalance is appropriate, in and of itself.

6.4 CONCLUSION

In the 1980s, greater capital mobility resulted from the increased global integration of international capital markets in the wake of worldwide financial liberalisation. This facilitated higher transnational capital flows which contributed to wider external imbalances.

In developing this argument, an extended national accounting framework was introduced which allowed sectoral balances to be presented systematically in macroeconomic terms. Mainstay theoretical models of the open economy were then critically surveyed and judged unsatisfactory as vehicles for explaining international capital transfer and external account determination. Alternatively, more meaningful capital-theoretic models of the external accounts linking saving, domestic investment and foreign investment were adapted to demonstrate the macroeconomic gains from international capital mobility and foreign investment.

This book has shown that a proper analysis of the determination of the external accounts under current conditions of highly mobile financial capital should acknowledge the gains from international trade in saving and that foreign investment has important real macroeconomic implications. It benefits some countries to lend excess saving to others and thereby run *CAS*s, at the same time as it benefits others with excess investment opportunities to borrow foreign saving and run *CAD*s. Foreign investment or capital account surpluses can indeed be beneficial, in a macroeconomic sense, for foreign funds help a nation expand its stock of productive capital. Focusing only on the corresponding trade and current account deficit and the cost of foreign capital in the external accounts is misleading and inevitably unpropitious.

Notes and References

1 Introduction

1. See McKinnon (1993) for extended discussion.
2. See also United Nations (1949).
3. See Edelstein (1982).
4. See Krugman (1989).

2 The External Accounting Framework

1. See also Gandolfo (1987).
2. In practice, apart from official intervention, the domestic currency value of official reserves may also be affected by exchange rate movements and gold price fluctuations. However, as with all other entries in this flow of funds framework, the change in reserves item abstracts from such capital gains and losses.
3. For expositional purposes, it is assumed here that private households save and private and public enterprises invest. However, in practice household expenditure on private dwellings is a significant component of private investment and retained earnings and undistributed income of enterprises comprise part of measured saving.
4. See United Nations (1968).
5. Consumer durables are included on the basis of Eisner's (1988) argument that these items yield a stream of benefits through time, even though they comprise a relatively small share of total assets. In Australia, for instance, consumer durables comprise only around 7 per cent of private wealth (Australian Treasury, 1991).
6. See International Monetary Fund (1983).

3 Traditional Approaches to the External Accounts

1. See Hinshaw (1945) and Chang (1946).
2. See Houthakker and Magee (1969), Artus and Knight (1984) and Goldstein and Khan (1985).
3. See Junz and Rhomberg (1973).

4. Other extensions of the tradable–non-tradable model include Corden (1982, 1985), Dornbusch (1980) and Prachowny (1984). Oppenheimer (1974) also notes the contribution of the Swedish economist Ohlin on this distinction, while Hinshaw (1975) recalls that Ricardo used the term 'home goods' to describe commodities which did not enter into world trade.

5. Major proponents of the MABP included Hahn (1959), Mundell (1968), Collery (1971), Dornbusch (1973), Mussa (1974), Frenkel and Johnson (1976), Fischer (1977) and Connolly (1978). For a survey, see Kreinin and Officer (1978).

6. See Johnson (1972) and Dornbusch (1973).

7. See, for instance Frenkel and Johnson (1978), Clements (1981) and Woo (1985).

8. Portfolio balance models of exchange rate determination were developed by McKinnon and Oates (1966), McKinnon (1969), Bryant and Hendershott (1970), Branson (1968, 1970, 1977), Hodjera (1971), Allen (1973), Kouri (1976), Girton and Henderson (1977), Allen and Kenen (1978) and Genberg and Kierzkowski (1979).

9. Kouri (1976), Dornbusch (1980) and Dornbusch and Fischer (1980).

10. Alternative expositions of the MF model are included in Dornbusch (1980), Frenkel and Razin (1987b), Marston (1985), Frenkel and Mussa (1985), MacDonald (1988) and Scarth (1988).

11. Dernburg (1989) adopts a similar approach.

12. For example, see Duesenberry (1949), Friedman (1957), Ando and Modigliani (1963), Modigliani (1970), Hall (1978), Hubbard and Judd (1986), Nelson (1987) and Abel (1990).

13. See Grossman (1972), Hayashi (1982), Hirschleifer (1958), Jorgenson (1971), Tobin (1969) and Abel (1990) some of which have open economy analogues to be considered in the next chapter.

14. Argy and Salop (1979) and Branson and Buiter (1983).

15. Also see Buiter and Miller (1981a, 1981b), Buiter and Purvis (1983) and Bruce and Purvis (1985).

16. Several extensions to the MF model suggested in the critique of this chapter are reflected in the econometric modelling of McKibbin and Sachs (1991).

4 Capital-theoretic Approaches to the External Accounts

1. See also Borts (1964), Amano (1965), Bardhan (1967), Neher (1970), Pitchford (1970), Onitsuka (1974), Negishi (1975), Ruffin (1979), Grubel (1987) and Niehans (1984).

2. Conventional trade theory concludes that, under certain conditions, including constant returns to scale, factor price equalisation can occur from trade in goods alone, without any trade in factors. Hence across-border equality of marginal products can exist before allowing capital movements.

3. If we allow for depreciation of the capital stock, the equilibrium return to capital becomes $f_k - d_e$ where d_e is the depreciation rate. This follows because $Y_n = f(K,L) - d_e K$ and with constant returns to scale

$$Y_n = (f_k(K,L) - d_e)K + f_L(K,L)L.$$

4. See Tobin (1969), Tobin and Brainard (1977), Yoshikawa (1980) and Hayashi (1982).

5. Intertemporal open economy models have also been exposited by Webb (1970), Razin and Svensson (1983), Sinn (1990), Sachs (1982), Buiter (1981), Obstfeld (1981), Dornbusch (1983), Corden (1985), Pitchford (1989), Frenkel and Razin (1987a, ch. 5) and Blanchard and Fischer (1989, ch. 2).

6. See Fama and Miller (1972) and Fama (1976).

7. See Frenkel and Razin (1987a).

5 Capital Mobility and the External Accounts

1. See Frankel (1979, 1983, 1985), Aliber (1980), Shafer and Loopesko (1983), Sachs (1983), Fukao and Hanazaki (1987), Fukao (1989), Lewis and Polasek (1990), Kupiec (1991), Miller and Weller (1991) and Blundell-Wignall and Browne (1991a, 1991b) for related discussion.

2. For related discussion, see Blanchard (1979), Blanchard and Watson (1982) and Summers (1986).

3. On this particular aspect, see Keynes (1936) ch. 12 for an extremely pessimistic interpretation.

4. See Dornbusch and Giovannini (1990).

5. See Frankel (1992).
6. See, for instance, Fieleke (1982), Feldstein (1983), Penati and Dooley (1984), Murphy (1984), and Dooley, Frankel and Mathieson (1987).
7. See Tobin (1983), Westphal (1983), and Bayoumi (1990).
8. Feldstein and Bacchetta (1989).
9. Blundell-Wignall and Browne (1991a, 1991b).
10. See Levich (1985).
11. See Hodjera (1973), Bryant (1975), Dooley and Isard (1980), Hansen and Hodrick (1980), Cumby and Obstfeld (1981), Bailey, Baillie and McMahon (1984) and Loopesko (1984).
12. See Mishkin (1984a, 1984b), Mark (1985) Cumby and Mishkin (1986), Gaab, Franziol and Horner (1986) and Frankel and MacArthur (1988).
13. See Monadjemi (1990) and Tease (1990).
14. See Caves (1971).
15. See Grubel (1968) and Solnik (1976, 1991).
16. See Lehmussaari (1990).
17. Dean *et al.* (1989) provide recent empirical evidence of this phenomenon ('seeing through the corporate veil') for OECD countries.
18. See Edey and Britten-Jones (1990) and Bosworth (1991).
19. See Agarwal (1980).
20. See Barro (1974, 1989), Buchanan (1976), O'Driscoll (1977) and Seater (1993).
21. Recent empirical tests of the 'twin deficits' hypothesis include Darrat (1988), Niskanen (1988), Zietz and Pemberton (1989) and Karunaratne (1992).

Bibliography

Abel, A.B. (1990), 'Consumption and Investment', in B.M. Friedman and F.H. Hahn (eds), *Handbook of Monetary Economics*, vol. 2, North-Holland, Amsterdam, ch. 14, 726–78.

Agarwal, J.P. (1980), 'Determinants of Foreign Direct Investment: A Survey', *Weltwirtschaftliches Archiv*, **116**(4), 739–73.

Alexander, S.S. (1952), 'Effects of a Devaluation on a Trade Balance', *International Monetary Fund Staff Papers* **1**(2), 263–78; reprinted in R.E. Caves and H.G. Johnson (eds) (1968), *A.E.A. Readings in International Economics*, vol. 11, Richard Irwin, Homewood, Illinois, 359–73.

Alexander, S.S. (1959), 'Effects of a Devaluation: A Simplified Synthesis of Elasticities and Absorption Approaches', *American Economic Review*, **49**(1), 22–42.

Aliber, R.Z. (1973), 'The Interest Parity Theory: A Reinterpretation', *Journal of Political Economy*, **81**(6), 1451–9.

Aliber, R.Z. (1980), 'The Integration of the Offshore and Domestic Banking System', *Journal of Monetary Economics*, **6**(4), 509–26.

Allen, P.R. (1973), 'A Portfolio Approach to International Capital Flows', *Journal of International Economics*, **3**, 135–60.

Allen, P.R. and Kenen, P.B. (1978), *Asset Markets, Exchange Rates, and Economic Integration: A Synthesis*, Cambridge University Press, Cambridge.

Amano, A. (1965), 'International Capital Movements and Economic Growth', *Kyklos*, **18**, 693–9.

Ando, A. and Modigliani, F. (1963), 'The Life Cycle Hypothesis of Saving: Aggregate Implications and Tests', *American Economic Review*, **53**(1), 55–84.

Argy, V. and Salop, J. (1979), 'Price and Output Effects of Monetary and Fiscal Policy under Flexible Exchange Rates', *IMF Staff Papers*, **26**(2), 224–56.

Artus, J. and Knight, M.D. (1984), 'Issues in the Assessment of the Exchange Rates of Industrial Countries', Occasional Paper no. 29, International Monetary Fund, Washington, DC.

Australian Treasury (1991), 'Private Sector Wealth', *Economic Round-Up* Summer, Australian Government Publishing Service, Canberra.

Bailey, M. (1957), 'Saving and the Rate of Interest', *Journal of Political Economy*, **65**(4), 279–305.

Bailey, R.W., Baillie, R.T. and McMahon, P.C. (1984), 'Interpreting Economic Evidence on Efficiency in the Foreign Exchange Market', *Oxford Economic Papers*, **36**, 67–85.

Balassa, B. (1964), 'The Purchasing Power Parity Doctrine: A Reappraisal', *Journal of Political Economy*, **72**(6), 584–96.

Bank for International Settlements (1989), *59th Annual Report*, BIS, Basle.

Bardhan, P.K. (1967), 'Optimum Foreign Borrowing', in K. Shell (ed.), *Essays on the Theory of Optimal Economic Growth*, MIT Press, Cambridge, Massachusetts, 117–28.

Barro, R.J. (1974), 'Are Government Bonds Net Wealth?', *Journal of Political Economy*, **82**(5), 1095–1117.

Barro, R.J. (1979), 'On the Determination of the Public Debt', *Journal of Political Economy*, **87**(5), 940–71.

Barro, R.J. (1989), 'The Ricardian Approach to Budget Deficits', *Journal of Economic Perspectives*, **3**, 37–54.

Bayoumi, T. (1990), 'Saving–Investment Correlations: Immobile Capital Government Policy or Endogenous Behaviour?', *IMF Staff Papers*, **37**(3), 361–87.

Bickerdike, C.F. (1920), 'The Instability of Foreign Exchange', *Economic Journal*, **30** (March), 118–22.

Blanchard, O.J. (1979), 'Speculative Bubbles, Crashes and Rational Expectations', *Economics Letters*, **4**, 387–9.

Blanchard, O.J. and Fischer, S. (1989), *Lectures on Macroeconomics*, MIT Press, Cambridge, Massachusetts, ch. 2, 37–90.

Blanchard, O.J. and Watson, M.W. (1982), 'Bubbles, Rational Expectations and Financial Markets', in P. Wachtel (ed.), *Crises in the Economic and Financial Structure*, Lexington Books, Lexington, Massachusetts, ch. 11, 295–315.

Blundell-Wignall, A. and Browne, F.X. (1991a), 'Increasing Financial Market Intergration, Real Exchange Rates and Macroeconomic Adjustment', OECD Working Papers, no. 96, February, OECD, Paris.

Blundell-Wignall, A. and Browne, F.X. (1991b), 'Macroeconomic Consequences of Financial Liberalisation', OECD Working Papers, no. 98, February, OECD, Paris.

Borts, G.H. (1964), 'A Theory of Long-Run International Capital Movements', *Journal of Political Economy*, **72**(3), 341–59.

Boskin, M. (1978), 'Taxation, Saving and the Rate of Interest', *Journal of Political Economy*, **86**(2), April, 513–27.

Bosworth, B.P., (1991), 'The Global Decline in Saving: Some International Comparisons', in P.J. Stemp (ed.), *Savings and Policy: Proceedings of a Conference*, Centre for Economic Policy Research, Australian National University, Canberra, 30–63.

Branson, W.H. (1968), *Financial Capital Flows in the US Balance of Payments*, North-Holland, Amsterdam.

Branson, W.H. (1970), 'Monetary Policy and the New View of International Capital Movements', *Brookings Papers on Economic Activity*, no. 2, 2355–62.

Branson, W.H. (1977), 'Asset Markets and Relative Prices in Exchange Rate Determination', *Sozialwissenschaftliche Annalen des Instituts für hohere Studien*, **1**, 69–89; reprinted as *Reprint in International Finance*, no. 20, Princeton University, New Jersey.

Bruce, N. and Purvis, D. (1985), 'The Specification of Goods and Factor Markets in Open Economy Macroeconomic Models', in R.W. Jones and P.B. Kenen (eds), *Handbook of International Economics*, vol. 2, North-Holland, Amsterdam, ch. 16, 807–57.

Bryant, R.C. and Hendershott, P.H. (1970), 'Financial Capital Flows in the Balance of Payments of the US: An Exploratory Empirical Study', *Princeton Studies in International Finance*, no. 25, Princeton University, New Jersey.

Buchanan, J.M. (1976), 'Barro on the Ricardian Equivalence Theorem', *Journal of Political Economy*, **84**(2), 337–42.

Buiter, W.H. (1981), 'Time Preference and International Lending in an Overlapping Generations Model', *Journal of Political Economy*, **89**(4), 769–97.

Buiter, W.H. and Miller, M.H. (1981a), 'Monetary Policy and International Competitiveness: The Problem of Adjustment', *Oxford Economic Papers*, **33**, 143–75.

Buiter, W.H. and Miller, M.H. (1981b), 'Real Exchange Rate Overshooting and the Output Costs of Bringing Down Inflation', *European Economic Review*, **18**, 83–130.

Buiter, W.H. and Purvis, D.D. (1983), 'Oil, Disinflation and Export Competitiveness: A Model of the "Dutch Disease"', in J. Bhandari and B.H. Putman (eds), *Economic Interdependence and Flexible Exchange Rates*, MIT Press, Cambridge, Massachusetts, ch. 8, 221–47.

Caves, R. (1971), 'International Corporations: The Industrial Economics of Foreign Investment', *Economica*, **38**, February, 1–27.

Chang, T.C. (1946), 'The British Demand for Imports in the Inter-War Period', *Economic Journal*, **56**, 188–207.

Clements, K. (1981), 'The Monetary Approach to Exchange Rate Determination: A Geometric Analysis', *Weltwirtschaftliches Archiv*, **117**(1), 20–25.

Collery, A. (1971), 'International Adjustment, Open Economies, and the Quantity Theory of Money', *Princeton Studies in International Finance*, no. 28, Princeton University, New Jersey.

Connolly, M. (1978), 'The Monetary Approach to an Open Economy: The Fundamental Theory', in B.H. Putnam and D.S. Wilford (eds), *The Monetary Approach to International Adjustment*, Praeger, New York, ch. 1, 6–18.

Corden, W.M. (1982), 'Exchange Rate Protection', in R.N. Cooper *et al.*, *The International Monetary System Under Flexible Exchange Rates*, Ballinger, Cambridge, Massachusetts.

Corden, W.M. (1985), *Inflation, Exchange Rates and the World Economy*, 3rd edn, Clarendon Press, Oxford.

Corden, W.M. (1991), 'Does the Current Account Matter? The Old View and the New', *Economic Papers*, **10**(3), 1–19.

Cumby, R.E. and Mishkin, F. (1986), 'The International Linkage of Real Interest Rates: The European–US Connection', *Journal of International Money and Finance*, **5**(1), 5–23.

Cumby, R.E. and Obstfeld, M. (1981), 'Exchange Rate Expectations and Nominal Interest Rates: A Test of the Fisher Hypothesis', *Journal of Finance*, **36**, 697–703.

Cumby, R.E. and Obstfeld, M. (1984), 'International Interest Rate and Price Level Linkages under Flexible Exchange Rates', in J. Bilson and R. Marston (eds), *Exchange Rate Theory and Practice*, University of Chicago Press, Chicago, ch. 3, 121–51.

Darrat, A.F. (1988), 'Have Large Budget Deficits Caused Rising Trade Deficits?', *Southern Economic Journal*, **54**(4), 879–87.

Dean, A., Durand, M., Fallon, J. and Hoeller, P. (1989), 'Saving Trends and Behaviour in OECD Countries', *OECD Working Papers*, no. 67, OECD, Paris.

Deane, P. (1978), *The Evolution of Economic Ideas*, Cambridge University Press, Cambridge.

Dernburg, T.F. (1989), *Global Macroeconomics*, Harper & Row, New York.

Dooley, M.P. and Isard, P. (1980), 'Capital Controls, Political Risk, and Deviations from Interest-Rate Parity', *Journal of Political Economy*, **88**(2), 370–84.

Dooley, M.P., Frankel, J.A. and Mathieson J. (1987), 'International Capital Mobility: What Do Saving–Investment Correlations Tell Us?', *IMF Staff Papers*, **34**(3), 503–30.

Dornbusch, R. (1973), 'Devaluation, Money and Non-Traded Goods', *American Economic Review*, **63**(5), 871–83.

Dornbusch, R. (1976a), 'Expectations and Exchange Rate Dynamics', *Journal of Political Economy*, **84**(6), 1161–76.

Dornbusch, R. (1976b), 'Exchange Rate Expectations and Monetary Policy', *Journal of International Economics*, **6**, 231–44.

Dornbusch, R. (1980), *Open Economy Macroeconomics*, Basic Books, New York.

Dornbusch, R. (1983), 'Real Interest Rates, Home Goods and Optimal External Borrowing', *Journal of Political Economy*, **91**(1), 141–53.

Dornbusch, R. (1986), 'Flexible Exchange Rates and Excess Capital Mobility', *Brookings Papers on Economic Activity*, no. 2, 209–26.

Dornbusch, R. and Fischer, S. (1980), 'Exchange Rates and the Current Account', *American Economic Review*, **70**(5), 960–71.

Dornbusch, R. and Giovannini, A. (1990), 'Monetary Policy in an Open Economy', in B.M. Friedman and F.H. Hahn (eds), *Handbook of Monetary Economics*, vol. 2, North-Holland, Amsterdam, ch. 23, 1231–1303.

Duesenberry, J.S. (1949), *Income, Saving and the Theory of Consumer Behavior*, Harvard University Press, Cambridge, Massachusetts.

Economic Report of the President (1987), Washington, DC, Government Printing Office.

Edelstein, M. (1982), *Overseas Investment in the Age of High Imperialism: The United Kingdom 1850–1914*, Columbia University Press, New York.

Edey, M. and Britten-Jones, M. (1990), 'Saving and Investment in S. Grenville (ed.), *The Australian Macroeconomy in the 1980's*, Reserve Bank of Australia, Sydney, 79–156.

Eisner, R. (1988), 'Extended Accounts for National Income and Product', *Journal of Economic Literature*, **26**(4), 1611–84.

Ethier, W. (1982), 'National and International Returns to Scale in the Modern Theory of International Trade', *American Economic Review*, **72**(3), 389–405.

Fama, E.F. (1976), *Foundations of Finance*, Basic Books, New York.

Fama, E.F. and Miller, M.H. (1972), *The Theory of Finance*, Holt, Rinehart & Winston, New York.

Feldstein, M. (1978), 'Comments and Discussion', *Brookings Papers on Economic Activity*, no. 3, 686–90.

Feldstein, M. (1983), 'Domestic Saving and International Capital Movements in the Long Run and the Short Run', *European Economic Review*, **21**, 129–51.

Feldstein, M. (1986), 'The Budget Deficit and the Dollar', *NBER Macroeconomics Annual*, National Bureau of Economic Research, Cambridge, Massachusetts, 355–409.

Feldstein, M. and Bacchetta, P. (1989), 'National Saving and International Investment', NBER Working Paper No. 3164, National Bureau of Economic Research, Cambridge, Massachussetts.

Feldstein, M. and Horioka, C. (1980), 'Domestic Saving and International Capital Flows', *Economic Journal*, **90**, June, 314–29.

Fieleke, N.S. (1982), 'National Saving and International Investment', *Saving and Government Policy*, Federal Reserve Bank of Boston Conference Series no. 25, Federal Reserve Bank of Boston, Boston, Massachusetts.

Fieleke, N.S. (ed.) (1989), *International Payments Imbalances in the 1980s*, Federal Reserve Bank of Boston, Boston, Massachusetts.

Fischer, S. (1977), 'Stability and Exchange Rate Systems in a Monetarist Model of the Balance of Payments', in R.Z. Aliber (ed.), *The Political Economy of Monetary Reform*, Macmillan, London, 59–73.

Fischer, S. and Frenkel, J.A. (1974), 'Interest Rate Equalisation and Patterns of Production, Trade and Consumption in a Two Country Model', *Economic Record*, **50**(4), 555–80.

Fisher, I. (1930), *The Theory of Interest*, Macmillan, New York.

Fishlow, A. (1988), 'External Borrowing and Debt Management', in R. Dornbusch and F. Helmers (eds), *The Open Economy: Tools for Policymakers in Developing Countries*, Oxford University Press, London, ch. 6, 187–222.

Fleming, J.M. (1962), 'Domestic Financial Policy Under Fixed and Under Floating Exchange Rates', *IMF Staff Papers*, **9**(3), 369–79.

Frankel, J.A. (1979), 'On the Mark: A Theory of Floating Exchange Rates Based on Interest Differentials', *American Economic Review*, **69**(4), 610–22.

Frankel, J.A. (1983), 'The Yen/Dollar Agreement: Liberalizing Japanese Capital Markets', Policy Analyses in International Economics, no. 9, Institute for International Economics, Washington, DC.

Frankel, J.A. (1985), 'International Capital Mobility and Crowding Out in the US Economy: Imperfect Integration of Financial Markets or of Goods Markets?', NBER Working Paper No. 1773, National Bureau of Economic Research, Cambridge, Massachusetts.

Frankel, J.A. (1992), 'Measuring International Capital Mobility', *American Economic Review*, **28**(2), 197–202.

Frankel, J.A. and MacArthur, A.T. (1988), 'Political vs Currency Premia in International Real Interest Rate Differentials', *European Economic Review*, **32**(5), 1081-1121.

Frenkel, J.A. (1976), 'A Monetary Approach to the Exchange Rate: Doctrinal Aspects and Empirical Evidence', *Scandinavian Journal of Economics*, **78**(2), 200–224.

Frenkel, J.A. and Johnson, H.G. (eds) (1976), *The Monetary Approach to the Balance of Payments*, Allen & Unwin, London.

Frenkel, J.A. and Johnson, H.G. (eds) (1978), *The Economics of Exchange Rates: Selected Studies*, Addison-Wesley, London.

Frenkel, J.A. and Mussa, M.L. (1985), 'Asset Markets, Exchange Rates and the Balance of Payments', in R.W. Jones and P.B. Kenen (eds), *Handbook of International Economics*, vol. 2, North-Holland, Amsterdam, ch. 14, 679–747.

Frenkel, J.A. and Razin, A.R. (1987a), *Fiscal Policies and the World Economy*, MIT Press, Cambridge, Massachusetts.

Frenkel, J.A. and Razin, A. (1987b), 'The Mundell–Fleming Model: A Quarter Century Later', *IMF Staff Papers*, **34**(4), 567–620.

Friedman, M. (1957), *A Theory of the Consumption Function*, Princeton University Press, New Jersey.

Fukao, M. (1989), 'Exchange Rate Fluctuations, Balance of Payments Imbalances and Internationalisation of Financial Markets', *Bank of Japan Monetary and Economic Studies*, **7**, February.

Fukao, M. and Hanazaki, M. (1987), 'The Internationalisation of Financial Markets', *OECD Economic Studies*, no. 8, 35–92.

Gaab, W., Franziol, M. and Horner, M. (1986), 'On Some International Parity Conditions: An Empirical Investigation', *European Economic Review*, **30**(3), 683–713.

Gandolfo, G. (1987) *International Economics: International Monetary Theory and Open Economy Macroeconomics*, Springer-Verlag, Berlin.

Gandolfo, H. and Swoboda, A.K. (1989), 'Policy and Current Account Determination Under Floating Exchange Rates', *IMF Staff Papers*, **36**(1), 1–30.

Genberg, H. and Kierzkowski, H. (1979), 'Impact and Long-run Effects of Economic Disturbances in a Dynamic Model of Exchange Rate Determination', *Weltwirtschaftliches Archiv*, **115**, 605–27.

Girton, L. and Henderson, W.L. (1977), 'Financial Capital Movements and Bank Behaviour in a Two-Country, Short-Run Portfolio Balance Model', *Journal of Monetary Economics*, **2**(1), 33–61.

Goldsmith, R.W. (1985), *Comparative National Balance Sheets: A Study of 20 Countries*, University of Chicago Press, Chicago.

Goldsmith, R.W. and Lipsey, R.E. (1963), *Studies in the National Balance Sheet of the United States*, Princeton University Press, New Jersey.

Goldstein, M. and Khan, M.S. (1985), 'Income and Price Effects in Foreign Trade', in R.W. Jones and P.B. Kenen (eds), *Handbook of International Economics*, vol. 2, North-Holland, Amsterdam, ch. 20, 1041–1105.

Grassman, S. (1980), 'The Long-Term Trends in Openness of National Economies', *Oxford Economic Papers*, **32**, 123–33.

Greenwood, J. (1983), 'Expectations, the Exchange Rate and the Current Account', *Journal of Monetary Economics*, **12**, 543–69.

Grossman, H. (1972), 'A Choice Theoretical Model of an Income-Investment Accelerator', *American Economic Review*, **62**(4), 630–541.

Grubel, H.G. (1968), 'Internationally Diversified Portfolios: Welfare Gains and Capital Flows', *American Economic Review*, **58**(5), 1299–1314.

Grubel, H.G. (1987), 'Foreign Investment', in J. Eatwell, M. Milgate and P. Newman (eds), *The New Palgrave Dictionary of Economics*, vol. 2, Macmillan, London, 403–6.

Hahn, F.H. (1959), 'The Balance of Payments in a Monetary Economy', *Review of Economic Studies*, **26**(1), 110–25.

Hall, R.E. (1978), 'Stochastic Implications of the Life-Cycle – Permanent Income Hypothesis: Theory and Evidence', *Journal of Political Economy*, **86**(6), 971–87.

Hansen, L. and Hodrick, R. (1980), 'Forward Exchange Rates as Optimal Predictors of Future Spot Rates', *Journal of Political Economy*, **80**(3), October, 829–53.

Harberger, A.C. (1950), 'Currency Depreciation, Income, and the Balance of Trade', *Journal of Political Economy*, **58**(1), 47–60.

Hayashi, F. (1982), 'Tobin's Marginal q and Average q: a Neo-Classical Interpretation', *Econometrica*, **50**(1), 213–24.

Hicks, J.R. (1937), 'Mr. Keynes and the "Classics"', *Econometrica*, **5**, 147–59; reprinted in J.R. Hicks (1967), *Critical Essays in Monetary Theory*, Clarendon Press, Oxford, ch. 7, 126–42.

Hicks, J.R. (1946), *Value and Capital*, Clarendon Press, Oxford.

Hinshaw, R. (1945), 'American Prosperity and the British Balance of Payments Problem', *Review of Economics and Statistics*, **27**(1), 4–9.

Hinshaw, R. (1975), 'Non-Traded Goods and the Balance of Payments', *Journal of Economic Literature*, **13**(2), 475–9.

Hirschleifer, J. (1958), 'On the Theory of Optimal Investment Decisions', *Journal of Political Economy*, **66**(5), 329–52.

Hodjera, Z. (1971), 'Short-Term Capital Movements of the United Kingdom, 1963–1967', *Journal of Political Economy*, **79**(4), 739–75.

Hodjera, Z. (1973), 'International Short-Term Capital Movements: A Survey of Theory and Empirical Analysis', *IMF Staff Papers*, no. 20, 683–740.

Houthakker, H.S. and Magee, S.P. (1969), 'Income and Price Elasticities in World Trade', *Review of Economics and Statistics*, **51**(2), 111–25.

Hubbard, R.G. and Judd, K.L. (1986), 'Liquidity Constraints, Fiscal Policy and Consumption', *Brookings Papers on Economic Activity*, no. 1, 1–50.

Hume, D. (1752), 'Of the Balance of Trade', in R.N. Cooper (ed.) (1989), *International Finance – Selected Readings*, Penguin, Harmondsworth, 25–37.

International Monetary Fund (1977), *The Monetary Approach to the Balance of Payments*, IMF, Washington, DC.

International Monetary Fund (1983), 'Statistical Asymmetry in Global Current Account Balances', *World Economic Outlook*, Supplementary Note 11, IMF, Washington, DC, 161–7.

International Monetary Fund (1988), *Exchange Arrangements and Exchange Restrictions: Annual Report*, IMF, Washington, DC.

International Monetary Fund (1989), *Economic Policy Co-Ordination: Proceedings of an International Seminar held in Hamburg*, IMF, Washington, DC.; HWWA-Institut für Wirtschaftsforschung-Hamburg, Hamburg.

International Monetary Fund, (1990), *World Economic Outlook*, IMF, Washington, DC.

Isard, P. (1977), 'How Far Can We Push the Law of One Price?', *American Economic Review*, **67**(5), 942–8.

Johnson, H.G. (1972), 'The Monetary Approach to Balance of Payments Theory', in H.G. Johnson, *Further Essays in Monetary Economics*, Allen & Unwin, London, ch. 9, 229–49.

Jorgenson, D.W. (1971), 'Econometric Studies of Investment Behaviour: A Survey', *Journal of Economic Literature*, **9**, 1111–47.

Jorgenson, D.W. and Grilliches, F. (1967), 'The Explanation of Productivity Change', *Review of Economic Studies*, **34**, July, 249–83.

Junz, H.B. and Rhomberg, R.R. (1973), 'Price Competitiveness in Export Trade Among Industrial Countries', *American Economic Review*, **63**(2), 412–18.

Karunaratne, N.D. (1992), 'The Twin Deficits Hypothesis in the Australian Context', *Economia Internazionale*, **44**(3), 1–23.

Kemp, M. (1962), 'Foreign Investment and the National Advantage', *Economic Record*, **38**(81), 56–62.

Kemp, M. (1966), 'The Gain from International Trade and Investment: A Neo-Heckscher–Ohlin Approach', *American Economic Review*, **56**(3), September, 788–809.

Kenen, P.B. (1985), 'Macroeconomic Theory and Policy: How the Closed Economy Was Opened', in R.W. Jones and P.B. Kenen (eds), *Handbook of International Economics*, vol. 2, North-Holland, Amsterdam, ch. 13, 625–77.

Keynes, J.M. (1936), *The General Theory of Employment, Interest and Money*, Macmillan, London.

Keynes, J.M. (1937), 'The Ex-ante Theory of the Rate of Interest', *Economic Journal*, **47**, December, 663–9.

Keynes, J.M. (1941), 'The Origins of the Clearing Union, 1940–1942', in *The Collected Writings of J.M. Keynes*, Macmillan, for the Royal Economic Society, London, vol. XXV, 1–144.

Kierzkowski, H. (1976), 'Theoretical Foundations of the Scandinavian Model of Inflation', *Manchester School of Economic and Social Studies*, **44**, 232–6.

Kindleberger, C.P. (1969), 'Measuring Equilibrium in the Balance of Payments', *Journal of Political Economy*, **77**(6), December, 873–91.

Kindleberger, C.P. (1987), *International Capital Movements*, Cambridge, University Press, Cambridge.

Kouri, P.J.K. (1976), 'The Exchange Rate and the Balance of Payments in the Short Run and in the Long Run: A Monetary Approach', *Scandinavian Journal of Economics*, **78**(2), 280–304.

Kreinin, M. and Officer, L. (1978), 'The Monetary Approach to the Balance of Payments: A Survey', *Princeton Studies in International Finance*, no. 43, Princeton University, New Jersey.

Krugman P.R. (1989), *Exchange Rate Instability*, MIT Press, Cambridge, Massachusetts.

Krugman, P.R. and Baldwin, R. (1987), 'The Persistence of the US Trade Deficit', *Brookings Papers on Economic Activity*, no. 1, 1–43.

Kupiec, P. (1991), 'Financial Liberalisation and International Trends in Stock, Corporate Bond and Foreign Exchange Market Volatilities', OECD Working Papers, no. 94, February, OECD, Paris.

Layton, A.P. and Makin, A.J. (1993), 'Estimates of the Macroeconomic Impact of Foreign Investment', *International Economic Journal*, **7**(4), 35–42.

Lehmussaari, OP. (1990), 'Deregulation and Consumption: Saving Dynamics in the Nordic Countries', *IMF Staff Papers*, **37**(1), 71–93.

Leiderman, L. and Blejer, M.I. (1988), 'Modeling and Testing Ricardian Equivalence: A Survey', *IMF Staff Papers*, **35**(1), 1–35.

Lerner, A.P. (1944), *The Economics of Control*, Macmillan, New York.

Levich, R.M. (1985), 'Empirical Studies of Exchange Rates', in R.W. Jones and P.B Kenen (eds), *Handbook of International Economics*, vol. 2, Cambridge, Massachusetts, 979–1040.

Lewis, M. and Polasek, M. (1990), 'Whither the Balance of Payments?', *Australian Economic Review*, **3**, 3rd Quarter, 5–16.

Loopesko, B. (1984), 'Relationships among Exchange Rates, Intervention and Interest Rates: An Empirical Investigation', *Journal of International Money and Finance*, **3**, 257–78.

MacDonald, R. (1988), *Floating Exchange Rates: Theories and Evidence*, Unwin Hyman, London.

MacDougall, G.D.A. (1960), 'The Benefits and Costs of Foreign Investment: A Theoretical Approach', *Economic Record*, Special Issue, **36**(73), 13–35.

Machlup, F. (1955), 'Relative Prices and Aggregate Spending in the Analysis of Devaluation', *American Economic Review*, **45**(3), 255–78.

Makin, A.J. (1988), 'Targeting Australia's Current Account: A New Mercantilism?', *Economic Analysis and Policy*, **18**(2), 199–212.

Makin, A.J. (1989a), 'Is the Current Account Deficit Sustainable?', *Australian Economic Review*, 2nd quarter, 29–33.

Makin, A.J. (1989b), 'Why Worry About the Capital Account Surplus?', *Policy*, **5**(4), 5–8.

Makin, A.J. (1989c), 'The External Imbalance: Burden or Blessing?', *The Australian Quarterly*, **61**(3), 337–43.

Makin, A.J. (1990), 'Wither the Balance of Payments', *Australian Economic Review*, 3rd quarter, 37–42.

Makin, A.J. (1992), 'Interventionism, Microeconomic Reform and the External Deficit', *Australian Economic Review*, 1st quarter, 15–21.

Makin, A.J. (1993), 'Capital Market Integration and National Wealth', *Australian Economic Review*, 2nd quater, 61–70.

Mark, N. (1985), 'Some Evidence on the International Inequality of Real Interest Rates', *Journal of International Money and Finance*, **4**, 189–208.

Markowitz, H. (1952), 'Portfolio Selection', *Journal of Finance*, **7**, 77–91.

Marshall, A. (1923) *Money, Credit and Commerce*, Macmillan, London.

Marston, R.C. (1985), 'Stabilization Policies in Open Economies', in R.W. Jones and P.B. Kenen (eds), *Handbook of International Economics*, vol. 2, North-Holland, Amsterdam, ch. 17, 859–916.

McKibbin, W. and Sachs, J.D. (1991) *Global Linkages*, Brookings Institution, Washington DC.

McKinnon, R.I. (1969), 'Portfolio Balance and International Payments Adjustment', in R.A. Mundell and A.K. Swoboda (eds), *Monetary Problems of the International Economy*, University of Chicago Press, Chicago, 199–234.

McKinnon, R.I. (1993), 'International Money in Historical Perspective', *Journal of Economic Literature*, **31**(1), 1–44.

McKinnon, R.I. and Oates, W. (1966), 'The Implications of International Economic Integration for Monetary, Fiscal and Exchange Rate Policy', *Princeton Studies in International Finance,* no. 16, Princeton University, New Jersey.

Meade, J.E. (1952), *The Theory of International Economic Policy, Volume I: Balance of Payments,* Oxford University Press, Oxford.

Miller, M. and Weller, P. (1991), 'Financial Liberalisation, Asset Prices and Exchange Rates', OECD Working Papers, no. 95, February, OECD, Paris.

Mishkin, F.S. (1984a), 'The Real Interest Rate: A Multi-Country Empirical Study', *Canadian Journal of Economics,* 17(2), 283–311.

Mishkin, F.S. (1984b), 'Are Real Interest Rates Equal Across Countries? An Empirical Investigation of International Parity Conditions', *Journal of Finance,* 39, 1345–58.

Modigliani, F. (1970), 'The Life Cycle Hypothesis of Saving and Intercountry Differences in the Saving Ratio', in W.A. Eltis, M.F.G. Scott and J.N. Wolfe (eds), *Induction, Growth and Trade: Essays in Honour of Sir Roy Harrod,* Clarendon Press, Oxford, 197–225.

Monadjemi, M.S. (1990), 'Testing the Degree of International Capital Mobility', *Australian Economic Papers,* no. 54, 29(4), 30–39.

Mun, T. (1664), *England's Treasure by Foreign Trade, or the Balance of Our Foreign Trade is the Rule of Our Treasure,* London.

Mundell, R.A. (1963), 'Capital Mobility and Stabilization Policy under Fixed and Flexible Exchange Rates', *Canadian Journal of Economics and Political Science,* 29, 475–85.

Mundell, R.A. (1968), *International Economics,* Macmillan, New York.

Murphy, R.G. (1984), 'Capital Mobility and the Relationship Between Saving and Investment in OECD Countries', *Journal of International Money and Finance,* 3, 327–42.

Mussa, M.L. (1974), 'A Monetary Approach to Balance of Payments Analysis', *Journal of Money, Credit and Banking,* 6, 333–51.

Negishi, T. (1975), 'Foreign Investment and the Long Run National Advantage', *Economic Record,* 31, 738–52.

Neher, P.A. (1970), 'International Capital Movements Along Growth Paths', *Economic Record,* 46, September, 393–401.

Nelson, C.R. (1987), 'A Reappraisal of Recent Tests of the Permanent Income Hypothesis', *Journal of Political Economy,* 95(3), 641–6.

Niehans, J. (1975), 'Some Doubts about the Efficacy of Monetary Policy Under Flexible Exchange Rates', *Journal of International Economics*, **5**(3), 278–81.

Niehans, J. (1977), 'Exchange Rate Dynamics With Stock-Flow Interaction', *Journal of Political Economy*, **85**(6), 1245–57.

Niehans, J. (1984), *International Monetary Economics*, Philip Allan, Oxford.

Niskanen, W. (1988), 'The Uneasy Relation Between the Budget and Trade Deficits', *Cato Journal*, **8**, 321–59.

Obstfeld, M. (1981), 'Macroeconomic Policy, Exchange Rate Dynamics and Optimal Asset Accumulation', *Journal of Political Economy*, **89**(6), 1142–61.

Obstfeld, M. (1986), 'Capital Mobility in the World Economy: Theory and Measurement', *Carnegie-Rochester Conference Series on Public Policy*, **24**, 55–104.

O'Driscoll, G.P. (1977), 'The Ricardian Non-Equivalence Theorem', *Journal of Political Economy*, **85**(1), 207–10.

Olson, M. and Bailey, M. (1981), 'Positive Time Preference', *Journal of Political Economy*, **80**(1), 1–25.

Onitsuka, Y. (1974), 'International Capital Movements and the Patterns of Economic Growth', *American Economic Review*, **64**(1), March, 24–36.

Oppenheimer, P.M. (1974), 'Non-Traded Goods and the Balance of Payments: An Historical Note', *Journal of Economic Literature*, **12**(3), 882–8.

Ostry, J.D. (1988) 'The Balance of Trade, Terms of Trade and the Real Exchange Rate', *IMF Staff Papers*, **34**(4), 541–73.

Penati, A. and Dooley, M. (1984), 'Current Imbalances and Capital Formation in Industrial Countries, 1949–81', *IMF Staff Papers*, **31**(1), 1–24.

Persson, T. and Svensson, L. (1985), 'Current Account Dynamics and the Terms of Trade', *Journal of Political Economy*, **93**(1), 43–65.

Pitchford, J.D. (1970), 'Foreign Investment and the National Advantage in a Dynamic Context', in I. McDougall and R. Snape (eds), *Studies in International Economics*, North-Holland, Amsterdam, ch. 11, 193–206.

Pitchford, J.D. (1989), 'Optimum Borrowings and the Current Account When There are Fluctuations in Income', *Journal of International Economics*, **26**, 345–58.

Pitchford, J.D. (1990), *Australia's Foreign Debt: Myths and Realities*, Allen & Unwin, Sydney.

Polak, J.J. (1957), 'Monetary Analysis of Income Formation and Payments Problems', *IMF Staff Papers*, **6**(1), 1–50.

Poterba, J.M. and Summers, L.H. (1987), 'Finite Lifetimes and the Savings Effects of Budget Deficits', *Journal of Monetary Economics*, **20**, 369–91.

Prachowny, M. (1984), *Macroeconomic Analysis for Small Open Economies*, Oxford University Press, Oxford.

Purvis, D.D. (1985), 'Public Sector Deficits, International Capital Movements, and the Domestic Economy: The Medium-Term is the Message', *Canadian Journal of Economics and Political Science*, **18**(4), 723–42.

Razin, A. and Svensson, L.E.O. (1983), 'The Current Account and the Optimal Government Debt', *Journal of International Money and Finance*, **2**, 215–24.

Robertson, D.H. (1940), *Essays in Monetary Theory*, P.S. King, London.

Robinson, J. (1937), 'The Foreign Exchanges', in J. Robinson (ed.), *Essays in the Theory of Employment*, Blackwell, Oxford.

Roll, E. (1961), *A History of Economic Thought*, Faber, London.

Ruffin, R.J. (1979), 'Growth and the Long-Run Theory of International Capital Movements', *American Economic Review*, **69**(5), 833–42.

Ruffin, R.J. (1984), 'International Factor Movements', in R.W. Jones and P.B. Kenen (eds), *Handbook of International Economics*, vol. 1, North-Holland, Amsterdam, ch. 5, 237–88.

Sachs, J.D. (1981), 'The Current Account and Macroeconomic Adjustment in the 1970s', *Brookings Papers on Economic Activity*, no. 1, 201–82.

Sachs, J.D. (1982), 'The Current Account in the Macroeconomic Process', *Scandinavian Journal of Economics*, **84**, 147–59.

Sachs, J.D. (1983a), 'Aspects of Current Account Behaviour of OECD Economies', in E. Claassen and P. Salin (eds), *Recent Issues in the Theory of Flexible Exchange Rates*, North-Holland, Amsterdam, 101–22.

Sachs, J.D. (1983b), 'Theoretical Issues in International Borrowing', *NBER Working Paper No. 1189*, National Bureau of Economic Research, Cambridge, Massachusetts.

Salop, J. and Spitaeller, E. (1980), 'Why Does the Current Account Matter?', *IMF Staff Papers*, **27**(2), 101–34.

Salter, W.E.G. (1959), 'Internal and External Balance: The Role of Expenditure and Price Effects', *Economic Record*, **35**(71), 226–38.

Scarth, W.M. (1988), *Macroeconomics: An Introduction to Advanced Methods*, Harcourt Brace Jovanovich, Toronto.

Seater, J.J. (1993), 'Ricardian Equivalence', *Journal of Economic Literature*, **31**(1), 142–90.

Shafer, J.R. and Loopesko, B. (1983), 'Floating Exchange Rates After Ten Years', *Brookings Papers on Economic Activity*, no. 1, 1–70.

Sinn, S. (1990), *Net External Asset Positions of 145 Countries: Estimation and Interpretation*, Kieler Studien 234, Institut für Weltwirtschaft an der Universität, Kiel.

Smith, A. (1776), *An Inquiry into the Nature and Causes of Wealth of Nations,* London.

Solnik, B. (1976), 'Why Not Diversify Internationally Rather Than Domestically?', *Financial Analysts Journal*, **30**, July–August, 39–53.

Solnik, B. (1991), *International Investments* 2nd edn, Addison-Wesley, Reading, Massachusetts.

Solow, R.M. (1956), 'A Contribution to the Theory of Economic Growth', *Quarterly Journal of Economics*, **70**, February, 65–94.

Stern, R.M. (1972), *The Balance of Payments*, Macmillan, Basingstoke.

Stockman, A.C. (1988), 'On the Roles of International Financial Markets and their Relevance for Economic Policy', *Journal of Money, Credit and Banking,* **20**(3), 531–49.

Summers, L.H. (1986), 'Does the Stock Market Rationally Reflect Fundamental Values?', *Journal of Finance*, **41**, 591–601.

Svensson, L.E.O. and Razin, A.R. (1983), 'The Terms of Trade, Spending and the Current Account: The Harberger–Laursen–Metzler Effect', *Journal of Political Economy*, **91**(1), 97–125.

Swan, T. (1955), 'Longer Run Problems of the Balance of Payments', paper presented at the Congress of the ANZAAS, Melbourne, published in H.W. Arndt and M.W. Corden (eds) (1963), *The Australian Economy: A Volume of Readings*, Cheshire Press, Melbourne, 384–95; reprinted in R.E. Caves and H.G. Johnson (eds) (1968), *A.E.A. Readings in International Economics*, vol. 11, Richard Irwin, Homewood, 455–64.

Swan, T. (1960), 'Economic Control in a Dependent Economy', *Economic Record*, **36**(73), 51–66.

Tease, W.J. (1990), 'The Balance of Payments', in S. Greville (ed.), *The Australian Macroeconomy in the 1980s*, Reserve Bank of Australia, Sydney, 159–221.

Tinbergen, J. (1952), *On the Theory of Economic Policy*, North-Holland, Amsterdam.

Tobin, J. (1955), 'A Dynamic Aggregative Model', *Journal of Political Economy*, **63**(2), 103–15.

Tobin, J. (1958), 'Liquidity Preference as Behavior Towards Risk', *Review of Economic Studies*, **25**, 65–86.

Tobin, J. (1969), 'A General Equilibrium Approach to Monetary Theory', *Journal of Money, Credit and Banking*, **1**(1), 15–29.

Tobin, J. (1978), 'A Proposal for International Monetary Reform', *Eastern Economic Journal*, **4**, July/October.

Tobin, J. (1983), 'Comments on Domestic Saving and International Capital Movements in the Long Run and the Short Run by M. Feldstein', *European Economic Review*, **21**, 153–6.

Tobin, J. (1984), 'On the Efficiency of the Financial System', *Lloyds Bank Review*, London, July, 1–15.

Tobin, J. and Brainard, W. (1977), 'Asset Markets and the Cost of Capital', in B. Balassa and R. Nelson (eds), *Economic Progress, Private Values and Public Policy*, North-Holland, Amsterdam, ch. 11, 235–63.

Tsiang, S.C. (1961), 'The Role of Money in Trade-Balance Stability: Synthesis of the Elasticity and Absorption Approaches', *American Economic Review*, **51**, 912–36.

Tsiang, S.C. (1989), 'Loanable Funds', in J. Eatwell, M. Milgate and P. Newman (eds), *The New Palgrave: Money*, Macmillan, London, 190–94.

Turnovsky, S.J. and Ball, K. (1983), 'Covered Interest Parity and Speculative Efficiency: Some Evidence for Australia', *Economic Record*, **59**, 271–80.

United Nations (1949), *International Capital Movements During the Inter-War Period*, United Nations, New York.

United Nations (1968), *A System of National Accounts*, Department of Economic and Social Affairs, United Nations, New York.

United Nations (1990), *United Nations Yearbook of International Trade Statistics*, United Nations, New York.

United Nations (various), *United Nations Monthly Bulletin of Statistics*, United Nations, New York.

Viner, J. (1937), *Studies in the Theory of International Trade*, Allen & Unwin, London.

Webb, L.R. (1970), 'The Role of International Capital Movements in Trade and Growth', in I. McDougall and R. Snape (eds), *Studies in International Economics*, North-Holland, Amsterdam, ch. 13, 225–66.

Westphal, U. (1983), 'Comments on Domestic Saving and International Capital Movements in the Long Run and the Short Run by M. Feldstein', *European Economic Review*, **21**, 157–9.

Woo, W.T, (1985), 'The Monetary Approach to Exchange Rate Determination Under Rational Expectations', *Journal of International Economics*, **18**, 1–16.

Yoshikawa, H. (1980), 'On the q Theory of Investment', *American Economic Review*, **70**(4), 739–43.

Zietz, J. and Pemberton, D.K. (1989), 'The US Budget and Trade Deficits: A Simultaneous Equation Model', *Southern Economic Journal*, **55**, 23–4.

Index

Index